NEOCLASSICAL FINANCE

PRINCETON LECTURES IN FINANCE

Yacine Ait-Sahalia, Series Editor

The Princeton Lectures in Finance, published by arrangement with the
Bendheim Center for Finance of Princeton University, are based on annual
lectures offered at Princeton University. Each year, the Bendheim Center
invites a leading figure in the field of finance to deliver a set of lectures on a
topic of major significance to researchers and professionals around the world.

Stephen A. Ross, *Neoclassical Finance*

NEOCLASSICAL FINANCE

STEPHEN A. ROSS

This work is published by arrangement with the
Bendheim Center for Finance of Princeton University

PRINCETON UNIVERSITY PRESS

PRINCETON AND OXFORD

Copyright © 2005 by Princeton University Press

Published by Princeton University Press, 41 William Street, Princeton, New Jersey

08540

In the United Kingdom: Princeton University Press, 3 Market Place, Woodstock,

Oxfordshire OX20 1SY

All Rights Reserved

Library of Congress Cataloging-in-Publication Data

Ross, Stephen A.

Neoclassical finance / Stephen A. Ross.

p.   cm. — (Princeton lectures in finance)

Includes bibliographical references and index.

ISBN 0-691-12138-9 (cloth : alk. paper)

1. Finance.   2. Efficient market theory.   I. Title.   II. Series.

HG173.R675   2004

332'.01—dc22   2004048901

British Library Cataloging-in-Publication Data is available

Printed on acid-free paoer. ∞

pup.princeton.edu

Printed in the United States of America

1 3 5 7 9 10 8 6 4 2

To Carol, Kate, Jon, Doug, Lucy
and my parents

CONTENTS

PREFACE

THIS MONOGRAPH IS based on the Princeton University Lectures in Finance that I gave in the spring of 2001. The Princeton lectures gave me a wonderful opportunity both to refine and expound on my views of modern finance. I hope this monograph will be interesting to those who know something about the subject and I hope that it can also serve as an entry point to the field for those with a serious interest in finance and a background in economics. This monograph will not, however, replace a textbook introduction; it is too idiosyncratic and personal to serve that purpose. Rather, the intention is that the reader will come to appreciate both the elegance and the power of neoclassical financial theory and analysis.

Unlike a textbook, this work leaves whole areas untouched or gives only a nod, for example, to corporate finance and option pricing in general and the binomial model in particular, which are treated as special cases of the absence of arbitrage. This is intentional, because I have used the occasion of these lectures to take a fresh modern look at some of the earliest themes of finance, such as efficient markets. I chose to do this out of a fear that in our zeal in economic theory to nail down the intricacies of game theoretic logic, which make it so difficult to make any general inferences about markets, we might inadvertently lose sight of the basic intuitions and the financial market data that we are trying to understand. In doing so, the afficionado will recognize that there are some new nuggets to be found in old mines.

The first chapter describes the main features of the theory. So as not to be consumed by historical reflection, the second chapter extends this work with some new results on the absence of arbitrage, which unify much of the research in this area by drawing on neoclassical consumer theory. It seemed appropriate to tie the basic theory of no arbitrage, which underlies most of modern finance, back to the foundations in consumer theory. More importantly, doing so proved quite fruitful because it opened up the possibility of closing a gap in the literature by providing a natural way to explore an upper bound to the volatility of the pricing kernel. The second chapter is more technically demanding than the rest of the book and can be skipped without harm by the reader who is prepared to accept its results, that are used in the third chapter. The third chapter examines the theory of efficient markets from the perspective of no arbitrage developed in the first lecture. Formalizing the neoclassical theory of efficient markets has proven to be elusive and the no-arbitrage setting provides a neat framework for doing so. The fourth and concluding chapter uses the previous development to examine a body of literature that looks at finance from a different perspective, the writings on behavioral finance. This chapter examines critically this alternative to traditional finance and offers a neoclassical explanation of a canonical paradox from this growing area, the so-called "Closed-End Fund Puzzle." While some may object to this chapter as an overly harsh indictment of the behavioral school of financial thinking, I must confess that it still represents much of my thinking on the subject.

There is not enough room here to remark on all of the people who have influenced me. I think the way I do because of them. Richard Roll has been a friend since I was just beginning in finance. Indeed, the second seminar in finance I ever attended was Dick talking about the term structure of interest rates. (The first was Fischer Black on the Black-Scholes model. Having been trained as a Bayesian, I made the proper and completely incorrect inference that Roll and Black were average representatives of financial researchers. Needless to say, the rest of the seminar had a difficult time meeting that expectation.) Dick's mastery of the basic intuitions of finance and his clarity of view remain signposts for me to this day. To John Cox I owe a lifetime of joint work and friendship and without him I never would have understood the deep inner structure of finance. Jon Ingersoll has also been a friend and colleague, and what I learned from him is the ubiquity of financial reasoning and a playful joy in its application in the most unexpected of venues. Mark Rubinstein's probing questions have always left me more informed than most people's answers. Of course, we all stand on the shoulders of giants, but what is particularly humbling is when my giants, those I've already noted along with Bob Merton, Myron Scholes, Gene Fama, and the late Fischer Black, are actually my peers. Bob defined much of the analytical framework that is the basic kitbag of modern finance; Myron, Fischer, and Bob, with their incredible insight—capsulized in the Black-Scholes model—started one of the great historical explosions of research. From both Dick and Gene's allegiance to the efficiency of markets, I acquired much of my own, and from them I also learned that the subject and the beliefs are science, not religion, and that one must always be ready to challenge them when the data is not agreeable to our prejudices. To this list I also want to add Sandy Grossman, whose marvelous work on the role of information in markets has changed the way we understand markets themselves.

Of course, no list would be complete without my students. I won't name them all, but I will note those with whom I have written. Anat Admati, Paul Pfleiderer, Mark Grinblatt, Chester Spatt, Michael Walsh, Will Goetzmann, Leonid Kogan, and some of the others I should have written with like Doug Diamond and John Campbell, all of whom taught me more than I ever taught them. I do, though, want to single out Phil Dybvig, who has been a frequent coauthor of mine. There is no one in finance from whom I have learned more than from Phil; his insight and understanding of our subject is unsurpassed, and much of the thinking in these lectures comes from him.

Thanks are due to many others for this work, including the wonderful colleagues I now have at MIT and, before that, at Yale and the Wharton School. I would particularly like to thank Jannette Papastaikoudi and Isil Erel for their creative inputs and their tireless efforts to correct my errors and analyze the data, and Dmitris Papanik, and John Geanakoplos for their careful readings. I also wish to thank Princeton University Press for giving me the opportunity to undertake this work and the Gamma Foundation for their generous support for the research on closed end funds. Despite all of these efforts, though, there are certainly errors and they are on my own account.

Finally, I want to thank my family, whose willingness to allow me to pursue my peculiar muse over many years is far more than I deserved.

NEOCLASSICAL FINANCE

ONE

NO ARBITRAGE:

THE FUNDAMENTAL THEOREM OF FINANCE

THIRTY YEARS AGO marked the publication of what has come to be known as the Fundamental Theorem of Finance and the discovery of risk-neutral pricing.[1] The earlier option pricing results of Black and Scholes (1973) and Merton (1973) were the catalyst for much of this work, and certainly one of the central themes of this research has been an effort to understand option pricing. History alone, then, makes the topic of these monographs—the neoclassical theory of finance—particularly appropriate. But, history aside, the basic theorem and its attendant results have unified our understanding of asset pricing and the theory of derivatives, and have generated an enormous literature that has had a significant impact on the world of financial practice.

Finance is about the valuation of cash flows that extend over time and are usually uncertain. The basic intuition that underlies valuation is the absence of arbitrage. An arbitrage opportunity is an investment strategy that guarantees a positive payoff in some contingency with no possibility of a negative payoff and with no initial net investment. In simple terms, an arbitrage opportunity is a money pump, and the canonical example is the opportunity to borrow at one rate and lend at a higher rate. Clearly individuals would want to take advantage of such an opportunity and would do so at unlimited scale. Equally clearly, such a disparity between the two rates cannot persist: by borrowing at the low rate and lending at the high rate, arbitragers will drive the rates together. The Fundamental Theorem derives the implications of the absence of such arbitrage opportunities.

It's been said that you can teach a parrot to be an economist if it can learn to say "supply and demand." Supply, demand, and equilibrium are the catchwords of economics, but finance, or, if one is being fancy, financial economics, has its own distinct vocabulary. Unlike labor economics, for example, which

[1] The central tenet of the Fundamental Theorem, that the absence of arbitrage is equivalent to the existence of a positive linear pricing operator (positive state space prices), first appeared in Ross (1973), where it was derived in a finite state space setting, and the first statement of risk neutral pricing appeared in Cox and Ross (1976a, 1976b). The Fundamental Theorem was extended to arbitrary spaces in Ross (1978) and in Harrison and Kreps (1979), who described risk-neutral pricing as a martingale expectation. Dybvig and Ross (1987) coined the terms "Fundamental Theorem" to describe these basic results and "Representation Theorem" to describe the principal equivalent forms for the pricing operator.

specializes the methodology and econometrics of supply, demand, and economic theory to problems in labor markets, neoclassical finance is qualitatively different and methodologically distinct. With its emphasis on the absence of arbitrage, neoclassical finance takes a step back from the requirement that the markets be in full equilibrium. While, as a formal matter, the methodology of neoclassical finance can be fitted into the framework of supply and demand, depending on the issue, doing so can be awkward and may not be especially useful. In this chapter we will eschew supply and demand and develop the methodology of finance as the implication of the absence of arbitrage.

No Arbitrage Theory: The Fundamental Theorem

The assumption of no arbitrage (NA) is compelling because it appeals to the most basic beliefs about human behavior, namely that there is someone who prefers having more wealth to having less. Since, save for some anthropologically interesting societies, a preference for wealth appears to be a ubiquitous human characteristic, it is certainly a minimalist requirement. NA is also a necessary condition for an equilibrium in the financial markets. If there is an arbitrage opportunity, then demand and supply for the assets involved would be infinite, which is inconsistent with equilibrium. The study of the implications of NA is the meat and potatoes of modern finance.

The early observations of the implications of NA were more specific than the general theory we will describe. The law of one price (LOP) is the most important of the special cases of NA, and it is the basis of the parity theory of forward exchange. The LOP holds that two assets with identical payoffs must sell for the same price. We can illustrate the LOP with a traditional example drawn from the theory of international finance. If s denotes the current spot price of the Euro in terms of dollars, and f denotes the currently quoted forward price of Euros one year in the future, then the LOP implies that there is a lockstep relation between these rates and the domestic interest rates in Europe and in the United States.

Consider individuals who enter into the following series of transactions. First, they loan \$1 out for one year at the domestic interest rate of r, resulting in a payment to them one year from now of $(1 + r)$. Simultaneously, they can enter into a forward contract guaranteeing that they will deliver Euros in one year. With f as the current one-year forward price of Euros, they can guarantee the delivery of

$$(1 + r)f$$

Euros in one year's time. Since this is the amount they will have in Euros in one year, they can borrow against this amount in Europe: letting the Euro interest rate be r_e, the amount they will be able to borrow is

$$\frac{(1+r)f}{(1+r_e)}.$$

Lastly, since the current spot price of Euros is s Euros per dollar, they can convert this amount into

$$\frac{(1+r)f}{(1+r_e)s}$$

dollars to be paid to them today.

This circle of lending domestically and borrowing abroad and using the forward and spot markets to exchange the currencies will be an arbitrage if the above amount differs from the \$1 with which the investor began. Hence, NA generally and the LOP in particular require that

$$(1+r)f = (1+r_e)s,$$

which is to say that having Euros a year from now by lending domestically and exchanging at the forward rate is equivalent to buying Euros in the current spot market and lending in the foreign bond market.

Not surprisingly, as a practical matter, the above parity equation holds nearly without exception in all of the foreign currency markets. In other words, at least for the outside observer, none of this kind of arbitrage is available. This lack of arbitrage is a consequence of the great liquidity and depth of these markets, which permit any perceived arbitrage opportunity to be exploited at arbitrary scale. It is, however, not unusual to come across apparent arbitrage opportunities of mispriced securities, typically when the securities themselves are only available in limited supply.[2]

While the LOP is a nice illustration of the power of assuming NA, it is somewhat misleading in that it does not fully capture the implications of removing arbitrage opportunities. Not all arbitrage possibilities involve two different positions with identical cash flows. Arbitrage also arises if it is possible to establish two equally costly positions, one of which has a greater set of cash flows in all circumstances than the other. To accommodate this possibility, we adopt the following framework and definitions. While the results we obtain are quite general and apply in an intertemporal setting, for ease of exposition we will focus on a one-period model in which decisions are made today, at date 0, and payoffs are

[2] I once was involved with a group that specialized in mortgage arbitrage, buying and selling the obscure and arcane pieces of mortgage paper stripped and created from government pass-through mortgages (pools of individual home mortgages). I recall one such piece—a special type of "IO"—which, after extensive analysis, we found would offer a three-year certain return of 37 percent per year. That was the good news. The bad news was that such investments are not scalable, and, in this case, we could buy only \$600,000 worth of it, which, given the high-priced talent we had employed, barely covered the cost of the analysis itself. The market found an equilibrium for these very good deals, where the cost of analyzing and accessing them, including the rents earned on the human capital employed, was just about offset by their apparent arbitrage returns.

received in the future at date 1. By assumption, nothing happens in between these two dates, and all decisions are undertaken at the initial date, 0.

To capture uncertainty, we will assume that there is a state space, Ω, and to keep the mathematics at a minimum, we will assume that there are only a finite number of possible states of nature:

$$\Omega = \{\theta_1, \ldots, \theta_m\}.$$

The state space, Ω, lists the mutually exclusive states of the world that can occur, m. In other words, at time 1 the uncertainty is resolved and the world is in one and only one of the m states of nature in Ω.

We will also assume that there are a finite number, n, of traded assets with a current price vector:

$$p = (p_1, \ldots, p_n).$$

Lastly, we will let

$$(\eta_1, \ldots, \eta_n)$$

denote an arbitrage portfolio formed by taking combinations of the n assets. Each element of η, say η_i, denotes the investment in asset i. Any such portfolio will have a cost,

$$p\eta = \sum_i p_i \eta_i,$$

and we will refer to such a combination, η, as an arbitrage portfolio if it has no positive cost,

$$p\eta \leq 0.$$

We represent the Arrow-Debreu tableau of possible security payoffs by

$$G = [g_{ij}] = [\text{payoff of security } j \text{ if state } \theta_{ij} \text{ occurs}].$$

The rows of G are states of nature and the columns are securities. Each row of the matrix, G, lists the payoffs of the n securities in that particular state of nature, and each column lists the payoffs of that particular security in the different states of nature.

With the previous notation, we can define an arbitrage opportunity.

Definition: An *arbitrage* opportunity is an arbitrage portfolio with no negative payoffs and with a positive payoff in some state of nature. Formally, an arbitrage opportunity is a portfolio, η, such that

$$p\eta \leq 0$$

and

$$G\eta > 0,$$

where at least one inequality for one component or the budget constraint is strict.[3]

We can simplify this notation and our definition of NA by defining the stacked matrix:

$$A = \begin{bmatrix} -p \\ G \end{bmatrix}.$$

Definition: An arbitrage is a portfolio, η, such that

$$A\eta > 0.$$

Formally, then, the definition of no arbitrage is the following.

Definition: The principle of *no arbitrage (NA)*:

$$NA \Leftrightarrow \{\eta \mid A\eta > 0\} = \varnothing,$$

that is, there are no arbitrage portfolios.

The preceding mathematics captures our most basic intuitions about the absence of arbitrage possibilities in financial markets. Put simply, it says that there is no portfolio, that is, no way of buying and selling the traded assets in the market so as to make money for sure without spending some today. Any portfolio of the assets that has a positive return no matter what the state of nature for the world in the future, must cost something today. With this definition we can state and prove the Fundamental Theorem of Finance.

The Fundamental Theorem of Finance: The following three statements are equivalent:

1. No Arbitrage (NA).
2. The existence of a positive linear pricing rule that prices all assets.
3. The existence of a (finite) optimal demand for some agent who prefers more to less.

Proof: The reader is referred to Dybvig and Ross (1987) for a complete proof and for related references. For our purposes it is sufficient to outline the argument. A linear pricing rule, q, is a linear operator that prices an asset when applied to that asset's payoffs. In this finite dimensional setup, a linear pricing rule is simply a member of the dual space, R^m and the requirement that

[3] We will use "$\geq$" to denote that each component is greater than or equal, "$>$" to denote that $\geq$ holds and at least one component is greater, and "$\gg$" to denote that each component is greater.

it is positive is just the requirement that $q \gg 0$. The statement that q prices the assets means simply that q satisfies the system of equations:

$$p = qG.$$

It is easy to show that a positive linear pricing operator precludes arbitrage. To see this let η be an arbitrage opportunity. Clearly,

$$0 \geq p\eta = (qG)\eta = q(G\eta).$$

But, since $q \gg 0$, this can only be true if

$$G\eta < 0,$$

which is inconsistent with arbitrage.

The converse result, that NA implies the existence of a positive linear pricing operator, q, is more sophisticated. Outlining the argument, we begin by observing that NA is equivalent to the statement that the set of net trades,

$$S = \{x \mid \exists \eta, \, x = A\eta\},$$

does not intersect the positive orthant since any such common point would be an arbitrage. Since S is a convex set, this allows us to apply a separating hyperplane theorem to find a y that separates S from the positive orthant, R^+. Since

$$yR^+ > 0,$$

we have $y \gg 0$. Similarly, for all η, we have

$$yS \leq 0 \Rightarrow yA\eta \leq 0 \Rightarrow yA\eta = 0$$

(since if the inequality is strict, $-\eta$ will violate it, i.e., S is a subspace.) Defining

$$q = (q_1, \ldots, q_m) = \frac{1}{y_1}(y_2, \ldots, y_{m+1})$$

implies that

$$p = qG,$$

hence q is the desired positive linear pricing operator that prices the marketed assets.

Relating NA to the individual maximization problem is a bit more straightforward and constructive. Since any agent solving an optimization problem would want to take advantage of an arbitrage opportunity and would want to do so at arbitrary scale, the existence of an arbitrage is incompatible with a finite demand. Conversely, given NA, we can take the positive linear pricing rule, q, and use it to define the marginal utility for a von Neumann-Morgenstern expected utility maximizer and, thereby, construct a concave monotone utility function that achieves a finite maximum.

$$\bullet \quad \bullet \quad \bullet \quad \bullet \quad \bullet$$

Much of modern finance takes place over time, a fact that is usually modeled with stochastic diffusion processes or with discrete processes such as the binomial. While our simplified statement of the Fundamental Theorem is inadequate for that setting, and while the theorem can be extended to infinite dimensional spaces, some problems do arise. However critical these difficulties are from a mathematical perspective, as a matter of economics their importance is not yet well understood. The nut of the difficulty appears to be that the operator that prices assets may not have a representation as a vector of prices for wealth in different states of nature, and that makes the usual economic analysis of trade-offs problematic.[4]

A *complete market* is one in which for every state θ_i there is a combination of the traded assets that is equivalent to a pure contingent state claim, in other words, a security with a payoff of the unit vector: one unit if a particular state occurs, and nothing otherwise. In a complete market G is of full-row rank, and the equation

$$p = qG$$

has a unique solution,

$$q = pG^{-1}.$$

This determinancy is one reason why market completeness is an important property for a financial market, and we will later discuss it in more detail. By contrast, in an *incomplete market*, the positive pricing operator will be indeterminate and, in our setting with m states and n securities, if $m > n$, then the operator will be an element of a subspace of dimensionality $m - n$. This is illustrated in figure 1.1 for the $m = 3$ state, $n = 2$ security example. In figure 1.1, each of the two securities has been normalized so that R^1 and R^2 represent their respective gross payoffs in each of the three states per dollar of investment.

The Representation Theorem

The positive linear operator that values assets in the Fundamental Theorem has several important alternative representations that permit useful restatements of the theorem itself.

---

[4] Mathematically speaking, separation theorems require that the set of net trades be "fat" in an appropriate sense, and in, say, the L^2 norm, the positive orthant lacks an interior. This prevents the application of basic separation theorems and requires some modifications to the definition of arbitrage and no arbitrage (see Ross [1978a], who extends the positive linear operator by finessing this problem, and Harrison and Kreps [1979], who find a way to resolve the problem).

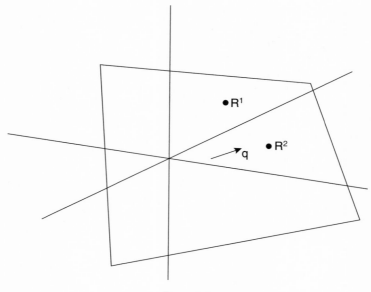

Figure 1.1

Definition: *Martingale* or *risk-neutral probabilities* are a set of probabilities, π^*, such that the value of any asset with payoffs of

$$z = (z_1, \ldots, z_m)$$

is given by the discounted expectation of its payoffs using the associated riskless rate to discount the expectation,

$$V(z) = \frac{1}{1+r} E^*[z] = \frac{1}{1+r} \sum \pi_i^* z_i.$$

Definition: A *state price density*, also known as a pricing *kernel*, is a vector,

$$\phi = (\phi_1, \ldots, \phi_m),$$

such that the value of any asset is given by

$$V(z) = E[\phi z] = \sum \pi_i \phi_i z_i.$$

These definitions provide alternative forms for the Fundamental Theorem.

Representation Theorem: The following statements are equivalent:

1. There exists a positive linear pricing rule.
2. The martingale property: the existence of positive risk-neutral probabilities and an associated riskless rate.
3. There exists a positive state price density or pricing kernel.

Proof:

$(1) \Leftrightarrow (2)$

From the Fundamental Theorem we know that there exists a positive pricing vector, $q \gg 0$, such that

$$V(z) = qz.$$

Consider, first, the sum of the q_i

$$V(e) = qe = \sum q_i.$$

We have written this as $V(e)$, where e is the vector of 1 since it is the value of receiving 1 for sure, that is, of getting 1 in each state. We can define a rate of return, r, as the return from investing in this security, thus,

$$r = \frac{1}{V(e)} - 1$$

or

$$V(e) = \frac{1}{1+r} = qe = \sum q_i.$$

Notice that r is uniquely defined if a riskless asset is traded explicitly or implicitly, that is, if e is in the span of the marketed assets.

Next we define the risk-neutral probabilities as

$$\pi_i{}^* = \frac{q_i}{\sum q_i} > 0.$$

Notice that, just as probabilities should, the $\pi_i{}^*$ sum to 1.

Hence, we have

$$V(z) = \sum q_i z_i = \left(\sum q_i \right) \sum \left(\frac{q_i}{\sum q_i} \right) z_i$$

$$= \left(\frac{1}{1+r} \right) \sum \pi_i^* z_i = \left(\frac{1}{1+r} \right) E^*[z],$$

where the symbol E^* denotes the expectation taken with respect to the risk-neutral probabilities (or "measure").

Conversely, if we have a set of positive risk-neutral probabilities and an associated riskless rate, r, it is clearly a positive linear operator on R_m, and we can simply define the state space price vector as

$$q_i = \left(\frac{1}{1+r}\right)\pi_i^* > 0.$$

(1) ⇔ (3)
Defining the positive state density as

$$\phi_i = \frac{q_i}{\pi_i} > 0,$$

we have

$$V(z) = \sum q_i z_i = \sum \pi_i \left(\frac{q_i}{\pi_i}\right) z_i$$
$$= \sum \pi_i \phi_i z_i = E[\phi z],$$

and the converse is immediate.

$$\bullet \ \bullet \ \bullet \ \bullet \ \bullet$$

Much of the research in modern finance has turned on extending these results into mathematically deeper terrain. The martingale, or risk-neutral, approach in particular has been the focus of much attention because of the ability to draw on the extensive probability literature. Interestingly, the risk-neutral approach was discovered independently of the Fundamental Theorem (see Cox and Ross 1976a, 1976b) in the context of option pricing, and only later was the relation between the two fully understood.

Given the tradition of Princeton in the physical sciences and given the role of finance as, perhaps, the most scientific of the social sciences, it is only appropriate to point out the close relation between these results and some fundamental results in physics. Without much imagination, the Representation Theorem can be formally stated in a general intertemporal setting in which a security with a random payoff, z_T, across time, T, has a current value, p, given by

$$p = E^*[e^{-\int_0^T r_s ds} z_T],$$

where r_s denotes the instantaneous risk-free interest rate and the asterisk denotes the expectation under the martingale measure. This is the usual modern statement of risk-neutral pricing. In this computation, the short interest rate can be stochastic, in which case all likely paths must be considered. More generally, too, the payoff itself could be path dependent as well. In practice, this expectation can be computed numerically by a summation over Monte Carlo simulations generated from the martingale measure. Such an integral, generated over paths, is equivalent to the Feynman-Kac integral of quantum mechanics.

Option Pricing

Black-Scholes-Merton

In the previously shown form, risk-neutral pricing (Cox and Ross 1976a, 1976b) provides the solution to the most famous and important examples of the implications of NA: the classic Black-Scholes-Merton (1973) option-pricing formula and the binomial formula of Cox, Ross, and Rubinstein (1979).[5] Without going into great detail, we will outline the argument.

The time T payoff for a call option on a stock with a terminal price of S_T at the option's maturity date, T, is:

$$C(S, T) = \max\{S_T - K, 0\},$$

where K is referred to as the strike or exercise price.[6] To compute the current value of the option we take the expectation of this payoff under the risk-neutral measure, that is, the martingale expectation. This is exactly the risk-neutral valuation that is obtained by assuming that the expected return on the stock is the risk-free interest rate, r, and taking the ordinary expectation.

The Black-Scholes model assumes that the stock process follows a lognormal distribution. In the formalism of Ito's stochastic calculus, this is written as

$$dS = \mu\,dt + \sigma dz,$$

where μ is the local drift or expected return, σ is the local speed or standard deviation, and the symbol dz is interpreted as a local Brownian process over the interval $[t, t + dt]$ with mean zero and variance dt. Assuming that the call option has a current value of $C(S, t)$, where we have written its arguments to emphasize the dependence of value on the current stock price, S, and the current time, t, and applying the integral valuation equation, we obtain

$$C(S, 0) = E^*[e^{-r(T - t)} \max\{S_T - K, 0\}].$$

The approach of Black and Scholes was less direct. Using the local equation, they observed that the return on the call, that is, the capital gain on the call, would be perfectly correlated locally with the stock since its value depends on

---

[5] See Black and Scholes (1973) and Merton (1973) for the original analysis with a diffusion process, and Cox, Ross, and Rubinstein (1979) for the binomial pricing model.

[6] We are assuming that the call is on a stock that pays no dividends and that it is a European call, which is to say that it can be exercised only at maturity and not before then.

the stock price. They used this result together with a local version of the Capital Asset Pricing Model (discussed later) to derive a differential equation that the call value would follow, the Black-Scholes differential equation:

$$\tfrac{1}{2}\sigma^2 S^2 C_{SS} + rSC_S + rC = -C_t.$$

Notice the remarkable fact that the assumed expected return on the stock, μ—so difficult to measure and surely a point of contention among experts— plays no role in determining the value of the call.

Merton pointed out that since the returns on the call were perfectly correlated with those on the underlying stock, a portfolio of the risk-free asset and the stock could be constructed at each point in time that would have identical returns to those on the call. To prevent arbitrage, then, a one-dollar investment in this replicating portfolio would be equivalent to a one-dollar investment in the call. The resulting algebra produces the same differential equation, and, as a consequence, there is no need to employ an asset-pricing model. Black and Scholes and Merton appealed to the literature on differential equations to find the solution to the boundary value problem with the terminal value equal to the payoff on the call at time T.

Cox and Ross observed that once it was known that arbitrage alone would determine the value of the call option, analysts were handing off the problem to the mathematicians prematurely. Since arbitrage determines the value, they argued that the value would be determined by what they called risk-neutral valuation, that is, by the application of the risk-neutral formula in the Representation Theorem. In fact, the Black-Scholes differential equation for the call value is the backward equation for the log-normal stochastic process applied to the risk-neutral expected discounted value integral, and, conversely, the discounted integral is the solution to the differential equation. The assumed expected return on the stock, μ, is irrelevant for valuation since in a risk-neutral world all assets have the riskless rate as their expected return.

It follows that the value is simply the discounted expected value of the terminal payoff under the assumption that the drift on the stock is the risk-free rate. Applying this analysis yields the famous Black-Scholes formula for the value of a call option:

$$C(S, 0) = SN(d_1) - e^{-rT} KN(d_2),$$

where $N(\cdot)$ denotes the standard cumulative normal distribution function and where

$$d_1 = \frac{\ln(S/K) + (r + \tfrac{1}{2}\sigma^2)T}{\sigma\sqrt{T}}$$

and

$$d_2 = d_1 - \sigma T.$$

The Binomial Model

The crucial features of the Black-Scholes-Merton analysis were not immediately apparent until the development of the binomial model by Cox, Ross, and Rubinstein. Was it the lognormal distribution, the continuity that allowed continuous trading or some other feature of the model, and would the analysis fall apart without these features? The binomial model resolved these questions, and because of its flexibility it has now become the preferred structure for valuing complex derivatives in the practical world of finance.

The binomial analysis is illustrated in figure 1.2. The value of the option at time t is given by $C(S, t)$ where we explicitly recognize its dependence on S, the stock price at time t. There are two states of nature at each time, t, state a and state b, representing the two possible futures for the stock price, aS or bS where $a > 1 + r > b$. The figure displays the gross returns on the three assets, $1 + r$ for the bond, a or b for the stock, and the formula $C(aS, t + 1)/C(S, t)$ for the option if state a occurs and $C(bS, t + 1)/C(S, t)$ if b occurs. With two states and three assets, one of the assets may be selected to be redundant, and this is represented by the line through the gross returns of the assets. The line is the combination of returns across the states, available by combining a unit investment in the three assets. To prevent arbitrage these three points must

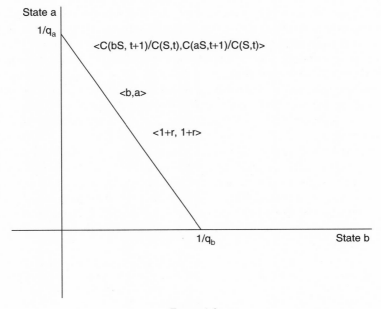

Figure 1.2

all lie on a line or else a portfolio of two of them would dominate the third. The equation of this line provides the fundamental difference equation, which can be solved subject to the boundary condition of the payoff at maturity, T, to give the current value of the option:

$$(1 + r)C(S, \tau) = \frac{1 + r - b}{a - b}C(aS, \tau - 1) + \frac{a - 1 + r}{a - b}C(bS, \tau - 1),$$

where τ is the number of periods left to maturity, $T - t$. The coefficients of the next period values in the equation are called the risk neutral probabilities for the binomial process, that is, they are the probabilities for the process under the assumption that the expected return is the risk-free rate. Notice that parallel with the absence of a role for the drift in the diffusion model, because the market is locally complete with two states and three assets, one of the assets is redundant and, given the values of the other two, the probabilities for the binomial jumps are not needed to value the third security. If we let the time difference between nodes grow small and increase in number so as to maintain a constant volatility for the stock return, this difference equation converges to the Black-Scholes differential equation.

Alternatively, we can derive the difference equation directly from the Fundamental Theorem by invoking NA directly to price a derivative security such as a call option. Since the stock and the option are perfectly correlated assets locally, we can form a portfolio of the two of them that is riskless, for example, we can short the stock and go long the option in just the correct proportions so as to eliminate all risk in the portfolio. Equivalently, we could construct a replicating portfolio composed of the risk-free rate and the stock whose return is locally identical to the return on the call option. NA in the form of the LOP requires that the portfolio, as a riskless asset, have the unique risk-free rate of return, r. The resulting equation is the discrete equation of the binomial model and the famous partial differential equation of Black and Scholes. In either case, the solution is the pricing equation derived from risk-neutral pricing.[7]

What, then, are the crucial features that allow for arbitrage to determine the price of the derivative security or option as a function of traded securities? Clearly, local spanning is sufficient (and except in unusual cases it is necessary) in the sense that the return of the derivative security must be a (locally) linear combination of the returns on the stock and any other marketed securities that are required to span its return. For example, if the volatility of the

[7] While the above is the most straightforward derivation, it is not the most powerful. In fact, there is no need to assume that the option inherits the stochastic properties of the underlying asset since it is possible to replicate the payoff of the option with a portfolio of the stock and the bond. Through NA this would force the value of the option to be the original cost of such a portfolio. See Ingersoll (1987) for this argument.

stock is itself random, then another instrument such as, say, the movement on a traded volatility index or on a market index that is perfectly correlated with changes in the volatility, would have to be used; and the value of the option would depend not only on the stock on which it was directly written, but also on the value of these other securities. As another example, we could have an option whose payoff depended not simply on the return of a single stock but rather on two or more assets, S and P with a payoff at time T of

$$S^2 + P.$$

In response to such complications, in discrete time the binomial might give way to a trinomial or an even more complex process (see Cox and Ross 1976a, 1976b).

Some Further Applications of the Representation Theorem

Asset Pricing

Historically and currently the pricing of assets has been a focus of neoclassical finance and, not surprisingly, a number of asset-pricing theories have been developed. While these differ in their form, they share some common intuitions. The theory of asset pricing began hundreds of years ago with a simple formulation drawn from the intuitions of gambling. The common sense view was that an asset would have a "fair" price if its expected return was simply the riskless rate,

$$E_i \equiv E[x_i] = r,$$

where x_i denotes the expected rate of return on asset i.[8] If this were so, then, on average, the asset would neither excessively reward nor penalize the holder.

With the work of Hicks and Samuelson and others, it was recognized that this was not an adequate representation. After all, individuals are generally assumed to be averse to risk and, therefore, assets whose returns are risky should command a lower price than riskless assets. This was captured by positing a return premium, π_i, for risky assets,

$$E_i = r + \pi_i,$$

where $\pi_i > 0$ to capture the need for additional return to compensate for risk.

Both theoretical and empirical works have focused on the determinants of the risk premium. Presumably π should be determined by two effects. On the one hand, the riskier the asset the greater the premium should be for bearing that risk and, on the other hand, the more averse investors are to risk, the greater the premium they would demand for bearing that risk. If we let risk

---

[8] This is usually credited to Bernoulli.

aversion be captured by a parameter, R, which could denote some average of the von Neumann-Morgenstern risk-aversion parameter for individual agents, and if we represent uncertainty by the simple variance of the asset return, σ^2, then we would have

$$\pi_i \propto R\sigma_i^2$$

with, perhaps, other factors such as asset supply and the like entering in.

It took decades from this initial set of concepts to the development of mean variance portfolio theory and the intuitive leap of the Capital Asset Pricing Model (CAPM) to recognize that this way of thinking about the risk premium was not quite correct. The contribution of modern neoclassical theory to this question comes with the recognition that since an asset fits into a portfolio, what matters for determining its risk premium is how it relates to the other assets in that portfolio, and not simply its overall volatility. We can illustrate this with a look at the three main asset-pricing theories.

Arbitrage Pricing Theory (APT)

The Arbitrage Pricing Theory (APT) is the most direct descendant of the Representation Theorem (see Ross 1973, 1976a). It begins with the simple observation that if one wants to say more about asset returns than can be obtained from arbitrage alone, one must make some assumptions about the distribution of returns. Suppose, then, we posit that returns follow an exact linear model,

$$x_i = E_i + \beta_i f,$$

where f is a common factor (or vector of factors) that influences the returns on all assets and β_i is the beta, or loading, for asset i on that factor. The vector f captures the innovations in the state variables that influence the returns of all the assets and, mathematically, in a static setting this is equivalent to a rank restriction on the matrix of returns.

Since all the assets are perfectly correlated, in this exact one-factor world we would expect the force of NA to dictate a pricing result. In fact, the logic is identical to that which we employed to derive the binomial pricing model for options. Since a unit investment in any asset gives a payoff equal to the gross return on that asset, the value of any gross return must be 1,

$$
\begin{aligned}
1 &= \frac{1}{1+r} E^*[1 + x_i] \\
&= \frac{1}{1+r}(1 + E^*[E_i + \beta_i f]) \\
&= \frac{1 + E_i + \beta_i E^*[f]}{1+r}.
\end{aligned}
$$

Rearranging the equation, we obtain the familiar statement of the risk premium, the Security Market Line (SML):

$$E_i - r = -E^*[f]\beta_i = \pi_f \beta_i,$$

where

$$\pi_f \equiv -E^*[f].$$

Observing from the SML that π_f is the risk premium on an asset with a beta of 1, we can rewrite the SML in the traditional form as

$$E_i - r = (E_f - r)\beta_i,$$

where E_f denotes the expected return on any portfolio with a beta of 1 on the factor. In other words, the risk premium depends on the beta of the asset that captures how the asset relates—or correlates—to the other assets through its relation to the common factor(s) and the premium, π_f, on those factor(s).

The exact specification of the foregoing statement is too stark for empirical practice because outside of option pricing and the world of derivative securities, assets such as stocks are not perfectly correlated and are subject to a host of idiosyncratic influences on their returns. We can modify the return generating mechanism to reflect this as

$$x_i = E_i + \beta_i f + \varepsilon_i,$$

where ε_i is assumed to capture the idiosyncratic, for example, company- or industry-specific forces on the return of asset i. If the idiosyncratic terms are sufficiently independent of each other, though, by the law of large numbers asymptotically as the number of assets in a well-diversified portfolio is increased, the portfolio return will approach the original exact specification. Such arguments lead to the SML holding in an approximate sense.[9]

While the intuition of the APT is clear, namely that factors exogenous to the market move returns and that pricing depends on them, and, further, that we can capture these by using endogenous variables such as those created by forming portfolios with unit loadings on the factors, exactly what these factors might be is unspecified by the theory. Next we turn to the traditional Capital Asset Pricing Model (CAPM) and its cousin, the Consumption Beta Model (CBM), to get more explicit statements about the SML.

---

[9] These conditions have led to a wide literature and some debate as to exactly how this return is accomplished and what is to be meant by an approximate pricing rule. See, for example, Shanken (1982) and Dybvig and Ross (1985).

The Capital Asset Pricing Model (CAPM) and the Consumption Beta Model (CBM)

Historically, the CAPM (Sharpe 1964; Lintner 1965) preceded the APT, but it is a bit less obvious what its relation is to NA. By assuming that returns are normally distributed (or locally normal in a continuous time-diffusion model), or by assuming that individuals all have quadratic utility functions, it is possible to develop a beautiful theory of asset pricing. In this theory two additional concepts emerge. First, since the only focus is on the mean and the variance of asset returns, individuals will choose portfolios that are mean-variance efficient, that is, portfolios that lie on the frontier in mean-variance space. This is equivalent to what is called two-fund separation (see Ross [1978b], who observes that all efficient portfolios lie on a line in the n-dimensional portfolio space). Second, a consequence of mean-variance efficiency is that the market portfolio, m, that is, the portfolio in which all assets are held in proportion to their values, will itself be mean-variance efficient. Indeed, the mean-variance efficiency of the market portfolio is equivalent to the CAPM.[10]

Not surprisingly, in any such model where valuation is by a quadratic, the pricing kernel will be in terms of marginal utilities or derivatives of a quadratic and will be linear in the market portfolio. It can be shown that the pricing kernel for the CAPM[11] has the form

$$\varphi = \frac{1}{1+r}[1 - \lambda(m - E_m)].$$

Hence any asset must satisfy

$$
\begin{aligned}
1 &= E[\varphi(1 + x_i)] \\
&= E\left[\left(\frac{1}{1+r}[1 - \lambda(m - E_m)](1 + x_i)\right)\right] \\
&= \frac{1 + E_i}{1+r} - \frac{\lambda}{1+r}\,\mathrm{cov}(x_i, m).
\end{aligned}
$$

Setting $i = m$, we can solve for λ,

$$E_m - r = \lambda\sigma_m^2,$$

---

[10] See Stephen Ross (1977). Richard Roll (1977) pointed out the difficulties that the potential inability to observe the entire market portfolio raises for testing the CAPM.

[11] The astute reader will recognize that this operator is not positive, and, therefore, the CAPM admits of arbitrage outside of the domain of assets to which the model is deliberately restricted. See Dybvig and Ingersoll (1982) for a discussion of these issues.

which allows us to rearrange the pricing equation to the SML:

$$E_i - r = \lambda \text{cov}(x_i, m)$$

$$= (E_m - r)\beta_i,$$

where β_i is the regression coefficient of asset i's returns on the market, m.

The SML verifies a powerful concept. Individuals who hold a portfolio will value assets for the marginal contributions they will make to that portfolio. If an asset has a positive beta with respect to that portfolio, then adding it into the portfolio will increase the volatility of the portfolio's returns. To compensate a risk-averse investor for this increase in volatility, in equilibrium such an asset must have a positive excess expected return, and the SML verifies that this excess return will, in fact, be proportional to the beta.

This is all valid in a one-period world where terminal wealth is all consumed and end-of-period consumption is the same as terminal wealth. Once we look at a multiperiod world, the possibility of intermediate consumption separates the stock of wealth from the flow of consumption. Not surprisingly, though, with a focus only on consumption and with a restriction that preferences depend only on the sum of the utilities of the consumption flow, the SML again holds, with β_i as the regression coefficient of asset i on individual or, when aggregation is possible, on aggregate consumption, and with the E_m interpreted as the expected return on a portfolio of assets that is perfectly correlated with consumption. This result is called the Consumption Beta Model (CBM) (see Merton 1971; Lucas 1978; and Breeden 1979).

More generally, in the next chapter we will exploit the fact that the Representation Theorem allows pricing to take the form of the security market line where the market portfolio is replaced by the pricing kernel, that is, excess expected return on assets above the risk-free return is proportional to their covariance with the pricing kernel. In a complete market where securities are traded contingent on all possible states and where agents have additive separable von Neumann-Morgenstern utility functions, individuals order their consumption across states inversely to the kernel, which implies that aggregate consumption is similarly ordered. This fact allows us to use aggregate consumption as a state variable for pricing and replaces covariance with the pricing kernel in the SML with covariance with aggregate consumption.

Corporate Finance

Corporate finance is the study of the structure and the valuation of the ownership claims on assets through various forms of business enterprise. The famous Modigliani-Miller (MM) Theorem (Modigliani and Miller 1958) on the irrelevance of the corporate financial structure for the value of the firm emerges as a corollary of the NA results. The MM Theorem is to modern corporate finance what the famous Arrow Impossibility Theorem is to the Theory of Social Choice. Like a great boulder in our path, it is too big to move and all of current research can be interpreted as an effort to circumvent its harsh implications. The MM Theorem teaches us that in the pristine environment of perfect markets with no frictions and no asymmetries in information, corporate finance is irrelevant. As with the Impossibility Theorem, appealing axioms have seemingly appalling consequences.

Consider a firm with an array of claims against its value. Typically we model these claims as debt securities to which the firm owes a determined schedule of payoffs with bankruptcy occurring if the firm cannot pay these claims in full. The residual claimant is equity, which receives the difference between the value of the firm at time 1 and the payoffs to the debt holders provided that the difference is positive, and which receives nothing if the firm is in bankruptcy. Notice that the equity claim is simply a call on the value of the firm with an exercise price equal to the sum of the face value of the debt claims. The statement of the MM Theorem, though, is much more general than this particular case.

The Modigliani-Miller (MM) Theorem: The value of a firm is independent of its financial structure.

Proof: Suppose a firm has a collection of claims against its value, with payoffs of $\langle z^1, \ldots, z^k \rangle$ at time 1. Since we have included all of the claimants, we must have

$$z^1 + \cdots + z^k = V_1.$$

As a consequence, at time 0 we have

$$\begin{aligned} \textit{value of firm} &= L(z^1) + \cdots + L(z^k) \\ &= L(z^1 + \cdots + z^k) \\ &= L(V_1), \end{aligned}$$

which is independent of the particulars of the individual claims.

• • • • •

Conclusion

There is, of course, much more to neoclassical finance than the material or even the topics presented in this chapter. We have omitted a detailed examination of individual portfolio theory and have hardly mentioned the fascinating intertemporal analysis of both individual optimal consumption and portfolio-choice problems as well as the attendant equilibria. We will rectify a small portion of this in the next chapter, but we will still not have time or space adequately to treat the intertemporal analysis. Having read that, though, a cynic might observe that almost all of contemporary intertemporal analysis is really just an extension of the static analysis of this chapter.

This coincidence occurs for two rather opposite reasons. On the one hand, most intertemporal models are simply sequences of one-period static models. With some rare exceptions, there are really no true intertemporal models in which consumption or production interacts over time in a fashion that is not additively separable into a sequence of static models. Secondly, a marvelous insight by Cox and Huang (1989) demonstrates that in a complete market the optimization and equilibrium problems may be treated as though the world were static—the integral view. If the market is complete, then any future pattern of consumption can be achieved by choosing a portfolio constructed from the array of state space-contingent securities. Such a portfolio will have a representation as a dynamic policy and it will produce the desired intertemporal consumption profile. In a sense, if the number of states of a static problem is augmented sufficiently, it can replicate the results of a complete intertemporal world. We will expand a bit on these issues in the next chapter.

TWO

BOUNDING THE PRICING KERNEL,

ASSET PRICING, AND COMPLETE MARKETS

THAT THE PRICING operator or, equivalently, its associated kernel, is positive and that it prices all assets, has a number of practical implications. Most applications begin by specifying the kernel as a projection onto the space of marketed assets. For example, projecting the kernel onto a risky asset (or more than one if necessary), we can then use the projection to obtain the parameters of the stochastic process for the kernel. From that parametrization we can price a derivative on that asset as the expected discounted value of the product of its payoffs and the kernel. According to the Representation Theorem, this is equivalent to risk-neutral pricing or pricing by the martingale measure.

By adding assumptions about preferences or technology we can further restrict the set of admissible pricing operators, but for now we want to see what, if any, additional implications we can derive about the kernel from NA alone. Interestingly, from the absence of arbitrage alone, it is possible to make some additional observations about the kernel beyond the fact that it exists and is positive.

Since assets are priced by the covariance between the kernel and their payoffs, the kernel must have enough variability to explain the cross-section of asset prices. If the kernel is insufficiently variable, then it will not have enough "reach" or "stretch" to price each of the marketed assets. To formalize this idea, let x be the excess return on a marketed asset: in other words, x is the return on an asset less the risk-free rate. Since this is the return on a position that borrows one unit at the risk-free rate and invests it in the asset, it uses no net wealth. According to NA, such a return must have zero value. If R denotes the gross return on the asset and r is the risk-free rate, then

$$x = R - (1 + r),$$

and NA implies that

$$
\begin{aligned}
0 &= value\ of\ excess\ return\ x \\
&= E[\phi x] \\
&= E[\phi]\,E[x] + \mathrm{cov}[\phi, x],
\end{aligned}
$$

which implies that

$$E[x] = -\left(\frac{1}{E[\phi]}\right)\mathrm{cov}[\phi, x].$$

Clearly, if the variability of the kernel is too low, then covariances with it will be too small to explain the cross-sectional spread over the space of marketed assets of the expected excess. Appealing to the Cauchy-Schwartz Inequality (or, equivalently, observing that correlations are between −1 and 1), we have

$$|E[x]| = \left(\frac{1}{E[\phi]}\right)|\text{cov}[\phi, x]| \le \left(\frac{1}{E[\phi]}\right)\sigma_\phi\sigma_x$$

producing the lower bound (Hansen and Jagannathan 1991)

$$\frac{\sigma_\phi}{E[\phi]} \ge \frac{E[x]}{\sigma_x} \equiv \frac{\mu_x}{\sigma_x}$$

on the volatility of the kernel. In this formulation, maximizing the right-hand side over all traded assets, x, we find the greatest lower bound to the volatility. If we additionally impose the constraint that the kernel not be negative, then we can tighten this bound further, albeit at the expense of a somewhat more elaborate construction. In other words, taking account of non-negativity will generally raise the lower bound.

A variety of researchers have extended these results and found other bounds. For example, Bansal and Lehmann (1997) show that the following bound must hold:

$$-E[\ln \phi] \ge \max_{\{\alpha|\alpha e=1\}} E[\ln \alpha R],$$

where e is the vector of ones, α is a portfolio of assets, and R is the vector of asset (gross) returns (in other words, minus the expectation of the log of the kernel is bounded above by the return on the portfolio that maximizes the expected rate of growth, i.e., the return on the growth-optimal portfolio). Since the log is concave, notice that this, too, is a form of bound on the volatility of the kernel, ϕ, and increasing the volatility of ϕ will lower the expectation. As we shall see, this and similar results (see, e.g., Snow 1991; Stutzer 1995; Cochrane and Saa'-Requejo 2000; and Bernardo and Ledoit 1999) all have a common origin.

The Kernel in Incomplete Markets

One important interpretation of the kernel is that it is the ratio of the marginal utilities at different wealth levels. The Arrow-Debreu prices are the marginal rates of substitutions for an investor in equilibrium, and the kernel is the set of rates of substitution per unit of probability. Hence, saying that the kernel has to be sufficiently volatile to price the marketed assets is equivalent to requiring that there be enough of a spread across marginal rates of substitution. For example, returning to the incomplete market illustrated in figure 1.1, the acceptable kernels can be visualized as hyperplanes that contain the space of marketed assets. In an m dimensional state space with n marketed assets, the acceptable hyperplanes lie in an $m - n$ dimensional subspace. This is illustrated in figure 1.1 with two asset returns in a three-dimensional space. The vector ϕ denotes the orthogonal to the hyperplane (where inner products are defined with respect to the expectation operator) and it is an acceptable kernel in the sense that it prices the assets and is positive.

Of course, if the market is complete, then the pricing operator is determined and is, for all practical purposes, unique. I don't know whether the market is complete or not, and, oddly, the question has become somewhat controversial. The debate is reminiscent of the old discussion over factor-price equalization in the pure theory of international trade. In a neoclassical trade model, if the number of traded goods is at least as great as the number of factors of production, then trade in goods—since it equalizes goods prices across countries and the mapping between costs and output prices is injective—will also equalize the factor prices in different countries. If the number of goods is less than the number of factors, then there will be an indeterminancy of dimension equal to the difference between them. Since the resulting equality is important for policy issues there was much discussion in the literature over whether the number of goods was larger, the same as, or less than the number of productive factors. Needless to say, this discussion went nowhere and was soon recognized as unresolvable.

Similarly, we can debate whether or not the marketed assets span the states and complete the markets, but there is no way to resolve the issue. I believe that, for all practical purposes, essentially all assets can be priced in the market by a combination of hedging and insurance—this will be expanded upon later. More importantly, since it is the distributions that matter (see Dybvig 1988), the states are merely a mathematical artifact used to display these returns as random variables; the state space is most usefully defined as the minimal set that will support the observed return distributions for the marketed assets. Generally, too, when we allow for derivative securities, spanning is greatly enhanced, and the ease with which this can be accomplished suggests that, at least for the marketed assets, all contingencies that are of concern to a sufficiently wealthy pool of agents will be available in the market.

To illustrate this point, consider a three-state example in which there is only one marketed asset, a stock with payoffs of $(1, 2, 3)$ in the three states. In this world, with only a single asset and three states, the market is clearly incomplete. But, suppose that we add to this world two new assets, a call with an exercise price of 1, $c(1)$, and a call with an exercise price of 2, $c(2)$. Now we have three assets and three states and, in fact, the Arrow-Debreu tableau of payoffs:

$$\begin{bmatrix} 1 & 0 & 0 \\ 2 & 1 & 0 \\ 3 & 2 & 1 \end{bmatrix},$$

where the first column displays the payoffs on the stock in the three states, the second column the payoffs on $c(1)$, and the third the payoffs on $c(2)$.[1] Since this tableau is of full rank, the market is now complete. This simple technique of adding options is replicated daily in the real markets of the world and nicely illustrates both the proximity of the theory to the markets as well as the ease with which important contingencies can be spanned by derivative assets.

Irrespective of completeness, though, because of data limitations we often observe and work with a subset of all of the assets, and it is useful to see what we can say about the pricing operator that is consistent with pricing on the subset. Operationally that is identical to assuming that the market is incomplete and, as a consequence, we might as well focus on what can be said about pricing in an incomplete market. Furthermore, whether or not the market is complete, we will assume that agents maximize their respective (von Neumann-Morgenstern expected) utilities by choosing their optimal combination or portfolio of the marketed assets, that is, some point in the space of marketed assets. At the optimum point there is a hyperplane or kernel that would support this choice in the sense that if we computed the marginal rates of substitution across wealth in the m dimensions at this point for a particular individual, those rates of substitution would then be an acceptable kernel. In figure 1.1 we could imagine some combination of the two assets and a concave preference ordering in the space that was tangent to the given hyperplane at that point. The gradient vector is the vector of marginal rates of substitution.

Interpreting the Kernel Bounds: NA and Neoclassical Consumer Theory

Now, suppose, we turn the analysis on its head and ask, what is the class of hyperplanes that could possibly be tangents to concave functions at points within the set of marketed assets? More precisely, we want to know what hyperplanes would be picked out by von Neumann-Morgenstern agents.

To make this formal, let M be the set of excess returns (i.e., returns net of the risk-free rate) of the marketed assets, and let Φ denote the admissible set of kernels (i.e., non-negative random variables that price the assets):

$$\Phi = \{\phi \mid \forall x \in M, E[\phi x] = 0\} \cap R^+,$$

[1] See Ross (1976b) for an exposition of this argument.

where R^+ denotes the non-negative orthant. A way of interpreting the literature on bounding the volatility of the kernel is that it provides an alternative way of characterizing Φ.

Given n marketed assets—we will call this set the "natural" market—that generate the marketed set, M, the agent has the problem of maximizing their preferences by choosing within M. If U is a monotone concave utility function (differentiable as required), then the agent chooses among portfolios, α, of the marketed assets. Letting x denote the vector of excess returns, with initial wealth, ω, the agent's wealth as a function of the portfolio choice is given by

$$w = \omega[(1+r) + \alpha x].$$

The agent's problem in this natural market is the following:

Problem 1:

$$\max_{\alpha} E[U(w)] = \max_{\alpha} E[U(\omega[(1+r) + \alpha x])],$$

which implies the necessary and sufficient first-order conditions at at an optimum,

$$E[U'(w)x] = 0.$$

By contrast: consider the agent solving the same problem in a complete market with the pricing kernel, ϕ.

Problem 2:

$$\max_{w} E[U(w)],$$

subject to the budget constraint

$$E[\varphi w] = \omega.$$

The first-order conditions for problem 2 are

$$U'(w) = \lambda \phi,$$

where λ is the marginal utility of wealth. Solving, we have

$$w = U'^{-1}(\lambda \phi),$$

which provides the familiar result that, at an optimum, wealth is monotone declining in the pricing kernel.

The solutions to these two formulations of the agent's optimization problem come together when, among the admissible pricing kernels, we choose the one that supports the solution to problem 1 using the marketed assets. In fact, if we simply take

$$\phi = \frac{U'(w)}{\lambda},$$

where w comes from problem 1, then this will be an admissible kernel since, by the first-order condition of problem 1, it correctly prices all of the assets (which is equivalent to assigning zero to the value of any excess return):

$$E[\phi x] = E\left[\frac{U'(w)}{\lambda}\right] = 0.$$

The comparison between problems 1 and 2 provides all of the bounds now available in the literature. Before showing this, though, it is useful to make an important connection between our problem and the traditional theory of consumer choice.

Problem 2 is the utility maximization problem with a separable objective function. This observation allows us to employ the familiar artillery of consumption theory to this somewhat unfamiliar terrain, and the result is an approach that can unify previous results. First, as in traditional consumer theory, we can define the indirect utility function and the expenditure function, respectively, as

$$V(\varphi, \omega) = \max_{\{w | E\{\varphi w\} = \omega\}} E[U(w)]$$

and

$$C(\varphi, u) = \min_{\{w | E[U(w)] \geq u\}} E[\varphi w].$$

The properties of V and C are well known. As would be expected, V is monotone decreasing in ϕ and C is monotone increasing in ϕ. More interestingly, C is concave in ϕ and V is quasiconvex. In addition, we have a minimax duality property. Letting ϕ^* denote the original state price-density and w^* the optimal solution at ϕ^*, the primal problem is

$$u^* = E[U(w^*)] = \min_{\{f | E[fw^*] \geq \omega\}} V(f, \omega),$$

which has as its solution, ϕ^*.

On the expenditure side,

$$\max_f C(f, u^*) - E[fw^*]$$

also has ϕ^* as its solution. Notice, too, that

$$\omega = C(\phi, V(\phi, \omega)),$$

and

$$u = V(\phi, C(\phi, u)),$$

and

$$E[\phi^* w^*] = \omega.$$

These results permit us to make some interesting observations about the pricing kernel. To begin with, they induce a partial ordering on the space of admissible kernels. Suppose that two kernels when viewed as random variables are related in the following way:

$$\phi' \cong \phi + \varepsilon,$$

where $\cong$ denotes that the left- and right-hand sides have the same marginal distribution, and where ε is a mean-zero random variable conditional on any realization of ϕ. This is simply the familiar statement of second-order stochastic dominance, that is, ϕ stochastically dominates ϕ'.

Perhaps, counter to first impressions, the stochastically dominated kernel is uniformly superior for any individual in the sense that it allows uniformly higher expected utility. The easiest way to see this is to observe that the optimal choice with the kernel ϕ is still feasible with the kernel ϕ', hence the optimal choice with ϕ' is at least as desirable as that with ϕ. Equivalently, we can use the concavity of the expenditure function

$$C(\phi, u) = E[\phi w_\phi^*] = E[(\phi + \varepsilon) w_\phi^*]$$
$$\geq E[(\phi + \varepsilon) w_{\phi + \varepsilon}^*] = C(\phi', u),$$

where we have indicated the dependence of the optimum wealth, w^*, on the pricing kernel. Since the cost is lower with the more variable kernel, the attainable utility is higher, which proves the following proposition:

Proposition 1: Given

$$\phi' \cong \phi + \varepsilon,$$

where

$$E[\varepsilon \,|\, \phi] = 0$$

for any utility function we have

$$V(\phi, \omega) \leq V(\phi', \omega)$$

and

$$C(\phi, u) \geq C(\phi', u)$$

Proof: See previous analyses.

· · · · ·

From the perspective of the agent, then, variability in the kernel is desirable. As a consequence, there is a lower limit to the variability of the kernel: If a kernel supports a particular agent's choice, then it must be sufficiently variable so as to permit the agent to attain at least the same level of utility that is achievable by direct investment in the marketed assets. Formally, we have

$$V_\phi = V(\phi, \omega) \geq \max_\alpha E[U(\omega[(1 + r) + \alpha x])] \equiv V_x.$$

This simple observation is the root of the various variance bounds in the literature. For example, choosing U to be quadratic,

$$U(w) = w - \frac{a}{2} w^2,$$

some manipulation reveals that

$$V_\phi = z - \frac{1}{2} z^2 + \frac{(1 - az)^2}{2a} \left[\frac{\sigma_\phi^2 (1 + r)^2}{\sigma_\phi^2 (1 + r)^2 + 1} \right]$$

$$\geq z - \frac{1}{2} z^2 + \frac{(1 - az)^2 \mu^2}{2a(\sigma^2 + \mu^2)}$$

$$= V_x,$$

where

$$z = (1 + r)\omega$$

and ω is the initial wealth. Some further manipulation yields

$$\frac{\sigma_\phi^2}{\mu_\phi^2} \geq \frac{\mu^2}{\sigma^2},$$

which is the familiar Hansen-Jagannathan (1991) bound.

Similarly, taking the utility function to be logarithmic, the optimum facing the kernel ϕ sets

$$U'(w) = \frac{1}{w} = \lambda \phi,$$

and, substituting into the budget constraint to solve for the multiplier, λ, we have

$$\lambda = \frac{1}{\omega},$$

hence

$$w = \frac{\omega}{\phi}$$

and

$$V_\phi = E[\ln(w(\phi))] = \ln\omega - E[\ln(\phi)].$$

Thus,

$$V_\phi = \ln\omega - E[\ln\phi] \geq \ln\omega - E[\ln(1 + R_G)] = V_x$$

or

$$E[\ln\phi] \leq - E[\ln(1 + R_G)],$$

where R_G is the growth optimal portfolio. This is the Bansal and Lehmann (1997) bound.

In a like fashion we can derive Snow's (1991) entropy bound, which is based on the exponential utility function and the gain/loss bound of Bernardo and Ledoit (1999), which can be derived from a bilinear utility function with a benchmark reference level. The latter is more complex, but the principle is the same.

Each of these choices for preferences generates a complete ordering of pricing kernels that separates the kernels into equivalence classes. For example, the quadratic utility function orders kernels by their standard deviations, σ_ϕ, and all kernels with the same standard deviation are in an equivalence class. The partial ordering by riskiness is consistent with this ordering in the sense that if one kernel has a lower standard deviation than another, then it cannot be riskier than the first in the partial ordering, that is, it is not equivalent to the first plus a mean-preserving spread.

We also have an interesting dual result with regard to the degree of risk aversion. Just as a "riskier" pricing kernel is more desirable in the sense that it lowers the cost of attaining the original utility level, so, too, a more risk-averse utility function requires more wealth to achieve the equivalent transformed utility. Letting U denote a concave, monotone utility function, by the Arrow-Pratt theorem (see Arrow 1965 and Pratt 1964), $G(U)$ is more risk averse than U if and only if G is a concave monotone transform. This leads to the following proposition:

Proposition 2:   The cost associated with $G(U)$ is at least as great as that of U,

$$C(\phi, u) \leq C(\phi, G(u))$$

Proof: By Jensen's inequality,

$$G(E[U(w)]) \geq E[G(U(w))];$$

hence, any wealth choice that allows

$$E[G(U(w))] \geq G(u)$$

also satisfies

$$G(E(U(w)]) \geq G(u),$$

which implies that

$$E[U(w)] \geq u.$$

Since any w that is feasible for the cost problem with utility function $G(U)$ is also feasible for the cost minimization with U, the proposition is proved.

• • • • •

Thus, as we consider more risk-averse utility functions, the cost of attaining the transformed utility level increases and we must use riskier kernels to offset this increase and achieve the original utility level. It is important to recognize, though, that we are not yet making any assumptions whatsoever about individual preferences. Rather, these concave utility functions are merely being used as mathematical tools for exploring the properties of the set of admissible kernels, Φ. For now, though, the fact that they are utility functions provides some valuable intuition, and we will later make use of their properties as representations of agent preferences.

Given these orderings and the lower bound imposed by the optimization problem in the natural market, it is only appropriate to ask whether there is also an upper bound to the kernel in terms of its riskiness. We will soon see that finding an upper bound is of great importance. The lower bounds we have found are all related in that they are bounds on attributes of the kernel which assure that the particular monotone concave preferences that generated them can support the optimal choice in the natural market. All the kernels that attain the bounds, or rather, that support their utility functions, are mutually neither dominated by nor dominant over any other kernel under the stochastic partial ordering.

Loosely speaking, an upper bound on the variability of the pricing kernel is a statement about how close particular opportunities can be to arbitrage opportunities. This was first proposed by Ross (1976a) and is explored further by Bernardo and Ledoit (1999) in their analysis of "good deals" and by Cochrane and Saa'-Requejo (2000). In what follows, building on the work of these authors, our framework allows us to analyze more precisely this interpretation of the "upper bound" argument.

An Upper Bound to the Volatility of the Pricing Kernel

From our previous two propositions, agents prefer kernels to be volatile, and more risk-averse agents require more variability. It follows, then, that any upper bound to the variability of the pricing kernel will be intimately related to an upper bound on the risk aversion of the marginal agent. Unfortunately, though, from the prices of assets alone it isn't possible to determine an upper bound to the variability of the kernel. If ϕ is any kernel that prices the traded assets correctly, then if ϕ' is stochastically dominated by ϕ and the noise that separates them is orthogonal to the asset returns, then ϕ' also correctly prices the assets.[2] In other words,

$$E[\varphi'x] = E[(\varphi + \varepsilon)x] = E[\varphi x] = 0.$$

An agent who faces the two kernels, however, would behave quite differently and, as we have shown, would prefer the riskier kernel.

Since any kernel can have its variability increased without affecting pricing, pricing considerations alone cannot put an upper bound on the volatility of the admissible kernels. In an incomplete market, the kernel is indeterminate and different agents will have different kernels supporting their optimal choices. The more risk averse the agent, the more variable will be the kernel that supports his given choice. Any one of these kernels correctly prices the assets and is non-negative, and each is a selection from the set of admissible kernels. On the other hand, if we restrict our attention to kernels that would be supported by investors in the market in the sense that some investor would have her optimal allocation at that kernel, then we can find a meaningful upper bound.

Suppose, then, that a utility function, U, is bounded above in risk aversion by another utility function, V. From the Arrow-Pratt theorem, then, we know that this is equivalent to V being a monotone, concave transform, G, of U. For example, if V is a constant relative-risk-aversion (CRRA) utility function with $R \neq 1$, then

$$\frac{w^{1-R}}{1-R} = G(U(w)),$$

where $G' > 0$ and $G'' < 0$.

The kernel associated with any utility function is given by

$$\phi_U = \mu_\phi \frac{U'(w)}{E[U'(w)]},$$

---

[2] The condition that the kernel be positive would impose further restrictions, but these would not generally be sufficient to bound the volatility (see Cochrane and Saa'-Requejo 2000). For example, the kernel consistent with a world containing a single asset that follows a continuous time lognormal distribution can have its volatility arbitrarily augmented without violating non-negativity.

where we will always assume a riskless asset and set

$$\mu_\phi = \frac{1}{1+r} \approx 1$$

for short time periods.

Our basic analytic tool will be the following relation between relative risk aversion and the volatility of the associated kernels.

Proposition 3: If a utility function, U, is bounded above in risk aversion by a utility function V, then

$$E[\phi_U^2] \le E[\phi_V^2].$$

Proof: From

$$V = G(U),$$

we have

$$
\begin{aligned}
E[\phi_V^2] &= \mu_\phi^2 \frac{E[V'^2]}{(E[V'])^2} = \mu_\phi^2 \frac{E[(G'U')^2]}{(E[G'U'])^2} \\
&= \frac{E[(G'U')^2](E[U'])^2}{(E[(G'U')])^2 E[U'^2]} \mu_\phi^2 \frac{E[U'^2]}{(E[U'])^2} \\
&= \frac{E[(G'U')^2](E[U'])^2}{(E[(G'U')])^2 E[U'^2]} E[\phi_U^2] \\
&= \kappa E[\phi_U^2].
\end{aligned}
$$

From the lemma in the appendix to this chapter we have

$$\kappa \ge 1,$$

hence

$$E[\phi_U^2] \le E[\phi_V^2].$$

$\bullet \quad \bullet \quad \bullet \quad \bullet \quad \bullet$

Proposition 3 allows us to bound the variance of any kernel generated by a utility function whose risk aversion is bounded. Simply to ease our computations and generate some parametric results, assume that the coefficient of relative risk aversion is uniformly bounded above by $R \ne 1$, and assume that the optimal wealth of the CRRA utility function is lognormally distributed:

$$\ln w \cong N(\mu, \sigma^2).$$

Thus,

$$E[w^c] = e^{c\mu + \frac{1}{2}c^2\sigma^2}$$

and, therefore,

$$E[\phi_U^2] \le E[\phi_R^2] = \mu_\phi^2 \frac{E[w^{-2R}]}{(E[w^{-R}])^2} = \mu_\phi^2 e^{R^2\sigma^2}.$$

Hence, since all kernels have the same mean, we obtain a bound on the volatility of the kernel in terms of the bound on risk aversion:

$$V[\phi_U] \le V[\phi_R] = \mu_\phi^2 e^{R^2\sigma^2} - \mu_\phi^2 \le \mu_\phi^2 R^2 \sigma^2,$$

where we have taken a linear approximation on the bound assuming that $(R\sigma)^2$ is small.[3]

Clearly, then, if we could uniformly bound all of the individual agents' coefficients of risk aversion or, alternatively, if we assumed the kernel was derived as the marginal utility of some aggregate measure of consumption or wealth, and if we could measue a bound to its risk: aversion coefficient, then we would have an upper bound on the volatility of the pricing kernel. Unfortunately, while sufficient, this is clearly too strong. Instead, we appeal to the standard quadratic or continuous time measure of aggregate risk aversion.

For each individual with a coefficient of risk aversion of R, his investment in risky assets can be approximated as

$$\alpha \approx \left(\frac{1}{R}\right)\frac{E_m - r}{\sigma_m^2},$$

where m is the common mean-variance efficient market portfolio, σ is its standard deviation, and E_m, denotes its mean return. Notice that the quadratic assumptions assure us of a local mean variance analysis.

Interestingly, this implies that the upper bound to the volatility of any agent's kernel is independent of her risk aversion. Agents with higher risk aversion have correspondingly lower allocations to the risky asset portfolio:

$$E[\varphi^2] \le R^2[\alpha^2 \sigma_m^2]$$
$$= R^2 \left(\frac{E_m - r}{R\sigma_m^2}\right)^2 \sigma_m^2 = \frac{(E_m - r)^2}{\sigma_m^2}.$$

[3] This expression is simply $R^2\sigma^2$ for short time-periods (as it is for continuous time-diffusions).

Weighting the individual holdings by the proportion of wealth held by each individual v, ω^v, summing and taking the aggregate supply of the risky asset to be unity, we obtain

$$\frac{E_m - r}{\sigma_m^2} \approx R \equiv \left(\sum \frac{\omega^v}{R^v} \right)^{-1},$$

where R is the measure of aggregate risk aversion in the market. The error in this neat approximation, however, is that it ignores the effects of hedging against changes in the future investment opportunity set.[4]

Now there are at least two possible perspectives we can take. First, we can view the market as incomplete and consider how this market risk-aversion would change with the introduction of new assets. There is little available here at a theoretical level, but common sense suggests that if the new assets are in zero net supply, it is unlikely that they will have an order-of-magnitude impact on the joint distribution of wealth proportions and risk-aversion coefficients. If they did have a large effect, then presumably it would have been in some agent's interest to have traded them, and they would already be part of the natural market. The implication, then, is that the foregoing would seem to be within an order of magnitude of a conservative estimate of the upper bound to risk aversion for the market. Alternatively, we could assume that the market is complete, perhaps with nascent new assets ready to enter at the slightest sign of interest on the part of market participants, and that it only appears incomplete because we observe a subset of the assets. In this interpretation, market incompleteness is an issue of observability rather than of a true lack of spanning assets. When we observe a new asset we are merely seeing something that was really there before, and there is no reason for aggregate market risk aversion to change at all. In either case, we now have the possibility of bounding the volatility of the pricing kernel by calculating a bound on market risk aversion.

Notice, too, that in either case we are computing the risk aversion at the margin and not the average risk aversion in the market. While the formula is an average, it is not a simple weighted average. Instead, it is the correct formula for computing the excess return that any asset must earn at the margin to be

[4] It is here where our static analysis is most dubious. In an intertemporal model, adjusting for discounting, kernel follows a martingale, and, in general, its local volatility will depend on the term above and, in addition, on the volatility of the state variables that drive returns (see Merton 1971). With a restriction to constant relative-risk-aversion utility, the volatility is actually additive in these two terms. The tendency of the portfolio position to offset the asset volatility remains, but the full exploration of this tendency still needs to be done. It is important to do so, and by ignoring it while we obtain some neat results, we also must acknowledge that there is much work to be done to verify their generality. However, for any model in which the pricing kernel is represented as a marginal utility of consumption or, more conservatively, of wealth, the analysis bounding the coefficient of relative risk aversion will be valid.

admitted into the market. To price an asset, then, we would evaluate its expectation under the martingale measure, where the measure can be taken to have a volatility bounded by the volatility bound formula following proposition 3 where R (or some conservative multiple of R) is employed. Notice, too, that the above aggregate $R \to 0$ as individual risk aversions approach 0 for a subset of agents with wealth bounded away from zero. In other words, the measure is clearly biased downward relative to a simple weighted average of risk aversions.[5] This offers the possibility that the resulting bound could be low enough to be useful—a result we will verify in the next chapter.

The analogy with consumer theory offers yet another interpretation of this bound. The range of possible volatilities of the kernel increases as we move from the most risk-tolerant investors to those that are the most risk averse. (We are referring to the cross-sectional volatility across the states for the hyperplane that supports their allocations.) From the appendix, in a lognormal diffusion market with a single risky market portfolio, if the standard deviation of the log of the pricing kernel is σ, then for an individual with the market average risk aversion, the wealth equivalent to a k-fold increase in the market R that determines the upper bound to the volatility of the kernel would be exponential in $(k^2 - 1)(\sigma^2/2R)$. With $k = 5$, $R = 2$, and $\sigma = .2$, this is equivalent to a more than doubling of initial wealth. In other words, if one believed that allocational inefficiency from the absence of complete markets is so great that the impact on equilibrium prices of completing the market would be equivalent to a fivefold increase in market risk aversion, then the resulting equilibrium would be one in which the average agent would be indifferent toward the choice between having more markets available and more than doubling her wealth—a highly unlikely possibility.

Concluding Calculations and Some Remarks about Consumption-Based Models and the Equity Risk Premium

We are left now with the task of measuring, R, the aggregate coefficient of relative risk aversion for the marginal investor. More precisely we want an upper bound to this coefficient. At this stage it is tempting to fall into the equity-risk-premium puzzle or "trap"—so it is worth pausing briefly to say something about this.

The consumption beta model (CBM) discussed in chapter 1 follows from the analysis we have displayed in this chapter (see Lucas 1978 and Breeden 1979; for empirical work, see Campbell and Cochrane 2000, and Lettau and Ludvigson

---

[5] This downward bias is also a simple consequence of Jensen's inequality.

2001). Formulated precisely, in a complete market, agents with additively separable utility functions share the same kernel and, as a consequence, both their individual consumption and aggregate consumption vary inversely with the kernel. This permits us to price assets in terms of their correlations with the growth of consumption—approximately in a discrete setting and exactly in an intertemporal diffusion model. The consumption beta model is marvelous theory but it surprises me that people take it as seriously as they do for empirical work.

Using the S&P 500 as the market—ignoring Roll's (1977) critique—the consumption beta theory implies that the market excess return is given by

$$E_{S\&P500} - r = (1+r)R(c_0)\sigma_g^2\beta_{S\&P500},$$

where the subscript g refers to the growth rate of consumption, c, where R is the coefficient of risk aversion of the utility of consumption, and where β is the regression beta of the S&P 500 on the rate of consumption growth.

We can use this information to solve for the risk aversion of the representative agent:

$$R(c_0) = \frac{E_{S\&P500} - r}{(1+r)\sigma_g^2\beta_{S\&P500}}.$$

Now for some back-of-the-envelope calculations. The equity risk premium of the S&P 500 over the risk-free rate has been about 5.5 percent from 1924 to the present, and the risk-free rate has averaged about 3.5 percent. The covariance of the S&P 500 with the growth rate of consumption from a simple regression is about 0.0014, and the standard deviation of the growth rate of consumption is about 3.5 percent. Putting this together we have

$$R(c_0) = \frac{E_{S\&P500} - r}{(1+r)\sigma_g^2\beta_{S\&P500}} = \frac{.055}{1.035 \times .0014} = 38,$$

which is ridiculously high, as was originally pointed out by Mehra and Prescott (1985), who dubbed this result the "Equity Premium Puzzle."

What seems so odd to me, however, is that anyone would expect to get a reasonable answer out of such a computation. It certainly is desirable to link the financial markets with the real markets, but there is no real hope for this particular effort. The theory requires that individuals rationally assess their opportunities across both time and states of nature and choose portfolios so as to set marginal rates of substitution equal to the prices, that is, to the kernel. Recalling the failures of early experiments with revealed preference and linear demand structures, these same individuals did nothing of the sort when they walked into a grocery and chose between Coca Cola and soap. If individuals don't behave rationally when they shop for goods at a point in time, then why would we expect that the much more complex computations required in finan-

cial markets would lead to results that were any more satisfactory? The suc-
cesses of finance have come precisely because it makes no such requirements
on individual rationality.[6]

By contrast, our computations don't require any allegiance to a consumption beta model or, for that matter, to any particular pricing model. The assertion of a limit on the risk aversion of the marginal investor is just a statement
about the desirability of an investment in the market at the margin. It is based
on the intuition that highly desirable investments will be accepted by the
market, and this same reasoning forms the basis for pricing insurance. We are
not aggregating individuals to get as representative investor, rather we are ask-
ing about the marginal investor. As such, it is appropriate to use the excess return on a portfolio of traded assets and not aggregate consumption.

Using the same analysis, we will just normalize by the variance of the S&P
500. With an annual standard deviation of about 20 percent, the revealed coefficient of risk aversion is

$$R = \frac{E_{S\&P500} - r}{(1+r)\sigma^2_{S\&P500}} = \frac{.055}{1.035 \times .04} = 1.3.$$

This is simply the computation of a price, or rather, the risk premium on the
index per unit of standard deviation. What would be a reasonable upper
bound, then? Without using much science, and guided by the discussion at the
end of the previous section, we will take the bound to be 5. As another ration-
ale, for a gamble with a standard deviation of 20 percent of wealth, an individual with a coefficient of 5 would pay an insurance premium on the order of

$$\tfrac{1}{2}R\sigma^2 = \tfrac{1}{2} \times 5 \times .04 = 10\%$$

of their wealth, which seems very high. More importantly, this is a potentially
empirically refutable statement about what risk premium the market will demand for an asset that is perfectly correlated with a given portfolio of mar-
ketable assets. We will use this result to good effect.

Combining our upper bound with the Hansen-Jagannathan bound, we have

$$\mu_\phi \frac{\mu_m}{\sigma_m} \le \sigma_\phi \le \mu_\phi R \sigma_m.$$

This statement, using the S&P 500 as the benchmark asset, m, produces with
annual data

$$27\% \le \sigma_\phi \le 96\%,$$

a lamentably large annual bound but one that we will refine in the next chapter.

---

[6] Here is where the advocates of the school of what is called behavioral finance and I share
common ground: we both have little confidence in individual rationality.

One last point. None of this should be construed as a defense of mean-variance analysis. In fact, we could have carried out exactly the same computations with a bilinear utility function and attained very similar results. Nor does any of the foregoing rest on the false belief that a high Sharpe ratio is the same as an arbitrage opportunity.[7] It is not, since a high variance and, therefore, a low Sharpe ratio can come about from a very highly skewed positive outcome and that would be good, not bad. Conversely, fixing the mean return, a high enough Sharpe ratio cannot be a bad deal. Rather, our analysis is consistent within the parametric assumptions that we have made, namely that the marginal utility function is uniformly bounded above in risk aversion, and the analysis is specifically designed to serve as a pragmatic guide for the problems that we will consider in the next chapter.

APPENDIX

Lemma: If x and y are positive random variables with y an increasing function of x, then

$$\kappa = \frac{E[x^2 y^2](E[y])^2}{(E[xy])^2 E[y^2]} \geq 1.$$

Proof: We must show that

$$\frac{E[x^2 y^2]}{E[y]^2} \geq \left(\frac{E[xy]}{E[y]} \right)^2.$$

To do so, we first show that

$$E[xq] \geq E[xs],$$

where

$$q = \frac{y^2}{E[y^2]}$$

and

$$s = \frac{y}{E[y]}.$$

---

[7] For any market index, m, the Sharpe ratio is simply

$$\frac{E_m - r}{\sigma_m}.$$

Notice that

$$E[q - s] = \frac{E[y^2]}{E[y^2]} - \frac{E[y]}{E[y]} = 0$$

and that as a function of y, $q - s$ is first negative and then positive with a single point at which it is zero. Since, by assumption, x is a positive and increasing function of y, it follows that

$$E[x(q - s)] \geq 0.$$

Hence,

$$\frac{E[xy^2]}{E[y^2]} \geq \frac{E[xy]}{E[y]}.$$

Defining a new measure by

$$E'[\cdot] = \frac{E[\cdot y^2]}{E[y^2]},$$

we can rewrite this result as

$$E'[x] \geq \frac{E[xy]}{E[y]}.$$

By the Cauchy-Schwartz inequality,

$$E'[x^2] \geq (E'[x])^2 \geq \left(\frac{E[xy]}{E[y]} \right)^2,$$

which is what we set about to prove.

• • • • •

Utility as a Function of the Volatility of the Kernel

For an agent with initial wealth of ω and a constant risk-aversion coefficient of R, facing a kernel ϕ with a volatility of σ^2, the optimal utility is

$$U = \frac{\left[\omega \exp\left(r + \frac{\sigma^2}{2R} \right) \right]^{1-R}}{1 - R}.$$

This implies that the indifference curves on which utility is held constant as ω and σ change are curves on which

$$\omega \exp\left(\frac{\sigma^2}{2R}\right)$$

is constant.

If we let a market average price of risk, R_w, set the volatility of the kernel, then from the previous results we have that

$$\sigma^2 = R_w^2 \sigma_w^2,$$

where σ_w denotes the volatility of wealth. Now a k-fold increase in R_w would accommodate a k-fold increase in the volatility of the kernel. The wealth increase that would be equivalent to this rise in the volatility for an agent with a risk aversion of R would be

$$\exp\left[(k^2 - 1)\left(\frac{\sigma^2}{2R}\right)\right] = \exp\left[(k^2 - 1)\left(\frac{R_w^2 \sigma_w^2}{2R}\right)\right].$$

THREE

EFFICIENT MARKETS

EFFICIENCY IS ONE of those words that is so appealing that we use it to describe many different phenomena. To an economist efficiency usually means "Pareto efficiency," which is a state of affairs where no individual's position can be improved without impairing another's, or "productive efficiency," which occurs when output cannot be increased for any one desirable good without lessening the production of another. In finance we refer to a market as efficient if it is informationally efficient. This is interpreted as saying that market prices incorporate all of the relevant information. Exactly what is meant by this attractive phrase is not entirely clear—nor is its relation to the other definitions of efficiency immediately apparent—but, roughly speaking, it is intended to convey the idea that since prices are the result of the decisions of individual agents, prices should therefore depend upon the information underlying those decisions. As a corollary, it should not be possible to attain superior returns by using the same information that the market possesses. Furthermore, it implies that the future returns on assets will largely depend not on the information currently possessed by the market but, rather, on new information that comes to the market, that is, on news. An investor whose information is the same or inferior to the information already incorporated into the prices will have no ability to predict the news and, therefore, no ability to outperform the market.

Pertinent to these issues, there is a large and fascinating literature on what is referred to as the No-Trade Theorem (see, e.g., Milgrom and Stokey 1982 or Tirole 1982). Assuming that markets are in an efficient ex ante equilibrium, that there are no noisy nonrational interferences with the setting of prices, and that the structure by which people acquire information is common knowledge even though their precise knowledge may be private, the No-Trade Theorem shows that it will not be possible to profit from your private information. Notice that the No-Trade Theorem goes further than market efficiency and argues that even if you do know something that others don't, you still cannot profit from that knowledge! The key to this result is that the method by which people acquire information is common knowledge, which roughly means that while someone else doesn't know what you know, they do know that you might know something useful and that you know that they know it, and so on. The No-Trade Theorem appeals to a cynicism familiar to finance: if someone wants to trade with me, they must think they can make money at my expense, and so why should I trade with them? Or, to put the matter another way: if there is common knowledge about the structure of the market, then any trade will reveal the initiating agent's knowledge and will be incorporated into market prices. Groucho Marx pithily captured this when he said that he wouldn't want to join any club that would have him as a member. The No-Trade Theorem provides a formal structure within which prices will reflect information—even privately held information—and within which individuals will not be able to prosper from this information.

As a matter of economic logic, though, markets cannot be perfectly efficient. If markets were perfectly efficient, then no one would have an incentive to act on their own information or to expend the effort to acquire and process information. It follows, then, that there must be some frictions in the market and some violations of market efficiency to induce individuals to acquire and employ information. Transactions costs and information-processing costs render many supposed violations of efficient markets ineffective, but financial markets are as close as we have to frictionless markets, and such imperfections seem a weak foundation for understanding how information is incorporated into prices. Alternatively, we can assume that markets are so incomplete that individuals do not have the ability to satisfy their demands to hedge their risks with each other and, as a consequence, retrading when information arrives offers new hedging possibilities. In the abstract, this assumption has its own problems and, as a practical matter, it is also not very satisfying. Currently, the preferred way to "end run" the No-Trade Theorem is by positing a "noisy rational expectations equilibrium model" that is populated both by the rational agents whom the No-Trade Theorem requires and also by irrational agents who transact for, say, random liquidity reasons as opposed to doing so to take advantage of profit opportunities. Unfortunately, though, at the heart of these models are some unsatisfactory parametric and, usually, quite cursory explanations of what forces drive individuals to engage in the "noisy" trades that prevent the market from fully revealing their information (see Grossman and Stiglitz 1980; Diamond and Verrecchia 1981; Grossman 1989; Kyle 1985; Admati and Pfleiderer 1988; DeLong, Shleifer, Summers, and Waldmann 1990). One troublesome problem is that noise has to be systematic, since individual and independent irrationality will simply diversify away in equilibrium. The real source of noise in the markets, be it unpredictable irrationality or some deeper forces such as an inability to perform the relevant computations, remains unknown and will not be easy to discover.

A full examination of these issues, however, would take us too far away from our main purpose, and we will have enough work to do just examining informational efficiency without attempting to defend it on the basis of some underlying equilibrium structure in markets. In fact, even making the appealing statement "prices capture information" precise enough for empirical work has proven to be very difficult (see, e.g., Fama's 1970 review or Cootner 1964; see also Fama, Fisher, Jensen, and Roll 1969). At the core of the attempt, though, lies some simple and critically important empirical characteristics of markets that we are attempting to understand. In particular, despite all of the efforts by academics, practitioners, and academic-practitioners to tickle some predictability out of financial market data, most would agree that the returns on financial assets are very close to being serially uncorrelated and are almost statistically unpredictable. In this chapter we will use the NA approach to develop a meta-neoclassical theory of efficient markets that abstracts from the foundational issues raised by the No-Trade Theorem, and we will use this development to interpret the empirical data and to assess the strengths and shortcomings of the theory.

For this work, it is most instructive to begin with the martingale or risk-neutral representation of the NA pricing framework. The price of an asset with next-period payoffs of z is

$$p = \frac{1}{1+r} E^* [z],$$

where the superscript $*$ indicates that the expectation is taken with respect to the risk-neutral probabilities rather than the natural probabilities.

To study efficient markets we must be explicit about the information set, S_t, which the market uses to condition expectations at time t, and that also requires us to be explicit about the timing of both when information is known and when values are determined. We will call S_t the market information set since it is the one that is used for price determination, and we will write

$$p_t = \frac{1}{1+r_t} E^* [z_{t+1} | S_t].$$

Fama (1970) proposed a number of candidates for the appropriate information set, and we will adopt his famous terminology.

Definition: Weak Form Efficiency. A market is said to be *weak form efficient* if S_t contains all of the past prices of the asset, that is, if

$$\{\ldots, p_{t-2}, p_{t-1}, p_t\} \in S_t.$$

Definition: Semi-Strong Form Efficiency. A market is said to be *semi-strong form efficient* if S_t contains all publicly available information, including past prices.

Since past prices are publicly available, semi-strong efficiency implies weak form efficiency. In addition, for semi-strong efficiency to hold, the market information set must include all past volume information as well as all other publicly available information such as government statistics, interest rates and their histories, and all accounting information about companies, such as their earnings and, more generally, their income statements and balance sheets.

Definition: Strong Form Efficiency.   A market is said to be *strong form efficient* if S_t contains all information.

Strong form efficiency requires the information set that determines prices to include not only the publicly available information but also the private information known only to some participants in the market. This means, for example, that when the foreman of the oil rig looks down and sees the first signs of oil in the exploratory well that the company is drilling, the price jumps on the stock exchange to reflect that information. Well, maybe the market doesn't react that quickly, but the real question is, who does the foreman call first, his boss or his stock broker?

The NA risk-neutral formulation of the theory of efficient markets bypasses some of the earlier controversies on the subject, and has some powerful implications.

Proposition 1:   If S_t denotes the market information set, then the value of any investment strategy that uses an information set $A_t \subseteq S_t$, is the value of the current investment.

Proof: Suppose that there are n assets whose terminal payoff will be

$$z = (z_1, \ldots, z_n),$$

and that an investment strategy consists of a portfolio

$$\alpha(A_t) = (\alpha_1(A_t), \ldots, \alpha_n(A_t)),$$

chosen at time t dependent upon the information set, A_t and costing $\alpha(A_t)p_t$ where p_t is the vector of the initial values of the assets. Since $A_t \subseteq S_t$, and since the current investment and the current interest rate, r_t, are elements of A_t, by the law of iterated expectations the value of the initial investment $\alpha(A_t)p_t$ in this strategy is given by

$$\frac{1}{1+r_t} E^*[z_\alpha | A_t] = \frac{1}{1+r_t} E^*[E^*[\alpha(A_t)z_{t+1} | S_t] | A_t]$$

$$= \frac{1}{1+r_t} E^*[\alpha(A_t)E^*[z_{t+1} | S_t] | A_t]$$

$$= \frac{1}{1+r_t} E^*[\alpha(A_t)(1+r_t)p_t | A_t]$$

$$= p_t$$

the initial investment.

• • • • •

Proposition 2:   If S_t denotes the market information set, then any investment strategy that uses an information set $A_t \subseteq S_t$, has a risk adjusted expected return equal to the interest rate, r_t.

Proof: The return on any investment strategy,

$$\alpha(A_t) = (\alpha_1(A_t), \ldots, \alpha_n(A_t)),$$

is given by

$$R_\alpha(t) = \frac{z_\alpha - \alpha p_t}{\alpha p_t} \equiv \frac{\alpha z - \alpha p_t}{\alpha p_t}.$$

The risk-adjusted expected return is the expectation under the martingale measure conditioning on A_t, and, from proposition 1,

$$
\begin{aligned}
E^*[R_\alpha(t)|A_t] &= E^*\left[E^*\left[\frac{z_\alpha - \alpha(A_t)p_t}{\alpha(A_t)p_t} \Big| S_t \right] \Big| A_t \right] \\
&= E^*\left[\frac{(1+r_t)\alpha(A_t)p_t - \alpha(A_t)p_t}{\alpha(A_t)p_t} \Big| A_t \right] \\
&= E^*[r_t | A_t] \\
&= r_t.
\end{aligned}
$$

• • • • •

Propositions 1 and 2 are powerful results that run counter to much of what many investors and some academic observers of financial markets believe. Consider an investor who trades on what is often called a reversal, or contrarian, strategy, purchasing stocks that have fallen in price for the past few months—"bargain hunting"—and selling securities whose prices have recently risen (see, e.g., Debondt and Thaler 1985, 1987; Chan 1988). Such a strategy is based on the past sequence of securities prices, hence, if it were successful, it would be a violation of weak form efficiency.

More sophisticated, yet, would be the securities analyst who carefully studied the accounting statements of firms as well as their past price histories and based investments on that analysis. If the market is semi-strong form efficient, then propositions 1 and 2 assert that such activities add no value and that their risk-adjusted returns are just the same as a risk-free investment in government bonds.[1]

---

[1] It is important to stress that it is the risk-adjusted returns that are ordinary, that is, they are equal to the market risk-free rate. Clearly such strategies can have more or less risk than, say, a strategy of just buying the market portfolio, but they will not add value simply by leveraging the market portfolio, for example, by moving along the capital market line in the CAPM.

If the market is strong form efficient then we have the truly discouraging result that no amount of information or analysis can add value in the financial markets since its already being used in the determination of market prices.

These are sobering consequences of the efficient market hypothesis and they lie at the root of the continuing debate between its supporters and its detractors. From the side of those engaged in the business of picking stocks, its no wonder that efficient market theory wins few friends. Further supporting the skeptics, while the bulk of the evidence is widely supportive, the ongoing empirical examination has thrown up a wide array of apparent anomalies which seem to provide excess profits and have fueled the interest in behavioral and other explanations. We will return to these issues, but it is interesting to note that amongst sophisticated practitioners there is a wide spread acceptance of the idea that markets are quite efficient. After all, we know from studies of mutual fund managers and the managers themselves know all too well that it is very difficult to 'beat the market'. Furthermore, some of the immediate consequences of the theory conform quite well to our observations of market returns. Consider the following result.

Proposition 3: Weak form efficiency implies that returns are serially uncorrelated over time and, indeed, that returns are uncorrelated with any linear combination of past returns when correlations are computed using the martingale probabilities.

Proof: This result follows from proposition 2. Let

$$L(p_{t-})$$

denote some linear combination of past prices. From proposition 2 we know that in the martingale measure the unconditional expected return is

$$E^*[R_t] = r_t.$$

From weak form efficiency, $L(p_{t-})$ is a subset of the market information set and, again applying Proposition 2, it yields

$$\text{cov}^*(R_t, L(p_{t-})) = E^*[(R_t - E^*[R_t])L(p_{t-})]$$

$$= E^*[E^*[(R_t - r_t)|L(p_{t-})]L(p_{t-})]$$

$$= E^*[(E^*[(R_t|L(p_{t-})] - r_t)L(p_{t-})]$$

$$= E^*[(r_t - r_t)L(p_{t-})]$$

$$= 0.$$

$$\bullet \quad \bullet \quad \bullet \quad \bullet \quad \bullet$$

As an example, if $L(p_{t-})$ is the lagged return on the asset

$$L(p_{t-}) = R_{t-k},$$

then proposition 3 would imply that

$$cov^*(R_t, R_{t-k}) = 0.$$

Unfortunately, though, the results of propositions 1, 2 and 3 are all in terms of the martingale measure, that is, they apply to risk-adjusted expectations. Empirical testing thus requires us to measure the risk-adjusted expectations presumably by employing a particular asset pricing model. In this sense, tests of either asset pricing models or the efficient market hypotheses are said to be joint tests of both the efficient markets hypothesis and the particular pricing model (see Fama 1970).

In a market where risk adjustments are expected to be small, though, these propositions would apply directly in terms of expectations. This would mean that proposition 3, for example, would simply assert that the serial correlation between current returns and any past prices or returns is zero under weak form efficiency.

What sort of markets would not have a significant risk premium effect? Clearly a market with little correlation to the rest of the economy, that is, to the systematic factors that explain risk premia in the APT or the CAPM or CBM. More generally, for any information set, A_t, that is a subset of the market information set and that contains the riskless asset, we have

$$E[R_t|A_t] = r_t + \lambda(A_t),$$

where $\lambda(A_t)$ is the risk premium and explicitly depends on A_t. In terms of the martingale measure,

$$E^*[R_t|A_t] = r_t = E[R_t|A_t] - \lambda(A_t),$$

that is, the risk-adjusted expectation:

$$cov(R_t, L(p_{t-})) = E[(R_t - E[R_t])L(p_{t-})]$$

$$= E[(E[(\lambda_t|L(p_{t-})] - E[(\lambda_t])L(p_{t-})]$$

$$= cov(\lambda_t, L(p_{t-})).$$

In other words, under weak form efficiency, the returns can be correlated with past prices only through the correlation of the risk premium with past prices. This gives us the following result:

Proposition 4:   Under weak form efficiency, if the risk premium is uncorrelated with past prices, then returns are uncorrelated with past prices.

Proof: See previous analysis.

• • • • •

In particular, then, we have the following:

Corollary: Under weak form efficiency, if the risk premium is deterministic, then returns are serially uncorrelated.

Proof: A special case of proposition 4.

• • • • •

More generally, then, if changes in expected excess returns (i.e., changes in the risk premium) are of second order in the period we are using, say, over the course of a day, then we would expect returns to be serially uncorrelated. For example, consider an asset whose expected excess return is 10 percent per year. This would be about three basis points ($\frac{3}{100}$ of 1%) per day. It would be unlikely for this expected return to move by more than, say, one or two basis points per day since that would be approximately a move of 3 to 6 percent per year in the expected return on the asset. On the other hand, the typical standard deviation of the asset could be about 40 percent per year, or about 40%/$\sqrt{365}$, 2.1 percent per day. In other words, the daily movement in the actual return is two orders of magnitude greater than any potential change in expected return.

Testing the Efficient Market Hypothesis and the Asset-Pricing Model

This rough calculation calls into the question the common assertion that all tests of the efficient market hypothesis are joint tests of efficient markets and of a particular asset pricing theory. To illustrate how these two hypotheses become intertwined, we have only to look at the enormous literature on what are called anomalies in asset pricing. We will examine some of these anomalies in greater detail in this and the next chapter, but for now consider the observation that stocks seem to display "momentum." A wide number of researchers (see, e.g., Jegadeesh and Titman 1993; Chan, Jagadeesh, and Lakonishok 1996; Lewellen 2002) have observed that a portfolio of stocks, chosen on the basis that over some time period—say, a year—they rose above what would have been expected given the movement in the market, will subsequently also outperform the market in the following month.[2]

A proper undertaking of any such test would seem to require the choice of a particular asset-pricing model. Without such a model it isn't possible to determine the risk premium, and therefore stocks that are chosen on the basis that they have outperformed other stocks and the market in general might continue to do so simply because they are riskier and *were* riskier during a sample period when risk was rewarded ex post. In that sense, there is no violation of the efficient markets hypothesis; it is merely an example of the observation that the expected return on riskier stocks—properly measured—is higher than that on less risky stocks. Any test, then, would appear to depend sensitively on whether the risk correction has been done properly, which means that it is a joint test of efficiency and the choice of an asset-pricing model.

This observation has led to something of a malaise in the testing of the efficient markets hypothesis. Typically the researcher makes some common adjustments for risk—for example, the Fama-French (1993) three-factor adjustment—and any anomalous results are generally taken as evidence against efficient markets. Of course, the advocates of efficiency can simply assert that the efficient markets hypothesis is unscathed and that what is in jeopardy is the asset-pricing model. At their most arch, opponents of this school of testing will thank the researcher for pointing out a necessary addition to the risk model. Irony aside, this is a very unsatisfactory state of affairs. Fortunately, though, the bounds on the volatility of the pricing kernel developed in the second chapter hold out the possibility of separating these two hypotheses.

In the original and classic tests, researchers often ignored correcting for risk or took it for granted that a simple market or index correction would be sufficient, and tested efficiency by assuming that pricing was risk neutral, that is, that the martingale probabilities were the actual natural probabilities. This assumption is quite typical—if implicit—in earlier studies of the efficient market hypothesis, and it is consistent with the rough calculation we made earlier. In weak form studies it is usually assumed that over short periods the actual volatility of returns dominates that of changes in the expected return, and thus such tests are traditionally conducted using a pure expectations hypothesis, that is, under risk neutrality. We will examine this assumption more closely, but before doing so it is worth discovering just how powerful a tool it is. There is no better place to look than Richard Roll's (1984) wonderful and classic examination of the efficiency of the orange juice futures market.

---

[2] There are many caveats to this simple description, for example, often the prediction period is "insulated" from the estimation period by one month. In other words, returns are estimated over, say, ten months, and then the portfolio that is formed on the basis of having the most momentum is then held for the twelfth month.

Orange Juice Futures Market and Noise

The efficient market hypothesis says that prices move because of news. They certainly don't move because of predictable or known changes in the information set. For example, suppose that a futures market for some commodity is semi-strong form efficient. That means that today's return should be uncorrelated with past news events, which have already been absorbed into the prices. A famous example comes from the orange juice futures market.

Orange juice is frozen as a concentrate, and there is a futures market that continuously quotes prices for these futures contracts throughout the day. The market opens at 9 A.M. and closes at 3 P.M. Monday through Friday. Consider Thursday's return as evaluated from the closing price on Wednesday to the closing price on Thursday. If the market is weak form efficient, then that return should be uncorrelated with Wednesday's return, which is measured from Tuesday's closing price to Wednesday's closing price:

$$\text{cov}(R_{Thu}, R_{Wed}) = \text{cov}\left(\left(\frac{p_{Thu} - p_{Wed}}{p_{Wed}}\right), \left(\frac{p_{Wed} - p_{Tue}}{p_{Tue}}\right)\right)$$
$$= 0.$$

It is widely accepted that the temperature is the most important variable in this market. As the temperature cools down at night, there is a risk of frost. Growers can take measures to mitigate this risk, but they still run the risk of losing the crop, which would raise prices significantly. The U.S. Weather Bureau publishes a forecast of the temperature at night. Indeed, they publish a rolling forecast, so that on Monday they will predict the minimum temperature for Thursday night and on Tuesday they will update this prediction. If the market is semi-strong form efficient, then these forecasts, F, will be incorporated into the price when the market closes on Wednesday, which implies that

$$\text{cov}(R_{Thu}, (F_{Thu|Tue} - F_{Thu|Mon})) = 0$$

We can test these propositions by simply regressing the current return on these past variables or by simply measuring the correlations. When we do so, we discover that the coefficients are not statistically different from zero. This is consistent with the hypothesis that the market is efficient and so is confirming of the hypothesis.

In fact, in these terms the case for efficient markets is even stronger. At the time these studies were first conducted, 90 percent of the oranges grown for frozen orange juice concentrate were grown within a ninety-mile radius of Orlando, Florida. (California oranges are too thick skinned to be used for concentrate.) The government maintains a very sophisticated weather forecasting operation involving satellites and the highest level imaging technology in Orlando, and it announces its forecast at 7 P.M. each day of the minimum temperature for that evening and the next two evenings. This is useful information because the growers can take steps to protect the crop if it's getting too cold or can even harvest it early. We have already seen that the market price incorporates this information, but there is something even more startling. Adjusting the 7 P.M. forecast downward when the market closing price at 3 P.M. is higher than the opening price that day, and upward when the market return is negative, actually improves the forecast. Not only does the market appear to incorporate all of the weather bureau's information, it actually seems to know something more!

But, there is more to this story than that. The regressions themselves have low power even when run with the return as the dependent variable and with past returns and weather forecasts as well as contemporaneous weather changes as the independent variables. The R^2 of these regressions is on the order of 1 or 2 percent. In other words, while there is no evidence that prices do not fully incorporate past information, we are pretty much at a loss to say why they move at all! If it's not weather—which is obviously the biggest determinant of supply changes—then what could it be? From my perspective, this lack of ex post explanatory power is one of the great puzzles of neoclassical finance. It is one thing to find that we cannot predict returns, but it is quite another to discover that we do not know what drove them after the fact. Presumably there is still private information that is relevant and has yet to be revealed, but this is only a presumption and certainly doesn't rise to the level of theory or explanation.

Event Studies—Using Efficient Market Theory

Because the efficient market hypothesis describes how information is reflected in prices, it is also the basis for some extremely useful techniques for using prices to examine the impact of particular types of news. Although the explanatory power of regressions of price changes on information is typically low, despite the noise, there is no doubt that market prices respond to information. The efficient market hypothesis argues that price movements reflect—indeed, fully reflect—the economic impact of information. This has led to the development of the *event study* as an important tool for using market return data to parse out the effects of particular events (see Fama, Fisher, Jensen, and Roll 1969; Brown and Warner 1985).

Suppose, for example, that we wish to determine the impact of stock issues on the price of stocks. When a publicly traded company sells stock, is that good news for the company or bad news? What about when the company changes its CEO or changes its corporate strategy or when a company announces an acquisition? The impact of all of these can and have been examined with event studies.

For a concrete example, suppose that company j announced on June 17, 2003, that it had made a promising discovery about a new cancer drug, and we wish to determine the effect of that news on the value of the company. Let us call June 17, 2003 the zero date, $t = 0$. The *cumulative returns* of the stock is

$$CR(t) = Cumulative\ Returns\ (t) = \sum_{t-10}^{t+10} R_\tau$$

during a twenty-day window—the event window—centered at that date. The cumulative returns are just the change in the price including dividend payments. Figure 3.1 is a stylized version of a plot in Fama, Fisher, Jensen, and Roll (1969) showing the cumulative returns for stocks in a window surrounding stock splits. Most event studies are conducted on a sample of firms and cover a particular event that they all experienced such as a stock offering or some type of news about their activities. In such cases, the zero dates are lined up and the cumulative returns are averaged over all of the firms as is displayed in figure 3.1. Notice that the stocks appear to have risen on the announcement day, but that is only the beginning of the story.

From figure 3.1 it appears that there was some leakage of the news before the announcement date. This can be seen from the rise in the cumulative returns. After the announcement, the news is in the public domain and, by semi-strong efficiency, we would not expect a statistically significant movement in prices from date 0 to date 10.

Of course, the announcement was not all that happened on that date. Presumably the market moved as well. If this stock has a beta on the market, then what we should really be examining is not the cumulative return but rather the *cumulative residuals*,

$$CRESID(t) = Cumulative\ Residuals\,(t) = \sum_{t-10}^{t+10} \varepsilon_\tau,$$

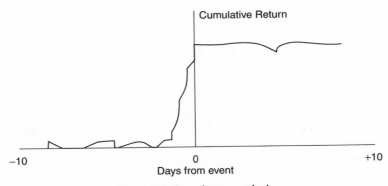

Figure 3.1 Cumulative residuals.

where

$$\varepsilon_t = R_t - (\beta_0 + \beta_m R_{mt})$$

is the residual from a regression of the returns, R_t, on the market returns, R_{mt}, with the betas as coefficients of the regression. Under the efficient market hypothesis, each residual measures the impact of news on that date. The cumulative returns over any period (ignoring compounding) is the change in value during that period, and the cumulative residuals over the period is the total change in value attributable to the events and news affecting the firm but not the overall market. In fact, figure 3.1 actually plots these cumulative residuals averaged over the sample of firms.

Furthermore, on each date there may well be news about the particular industry, the drug industry in this example, and that, too, would effect the returns. To isolate the impact of the announcement we should also eliminate that effect. If I_t is the return at date t on an index of industry stocks, then the residual on the date would be changed to

$$\varepsilon_t = R_t - (\beta_0 + \beta_m R_{mt} + \beta_I R_{It}).$$

Under the semi-strong hypothesis of market efficiency, conditional on the information at any date t, we should have

$$E[\varepsilon_t \mid R_{mt}, R_{It}] = E[R_t - (\beta_0 + \beta_m R_{mt} + \beta_I R_{It}) \mid R_{mt}, R_{It}] = 0,$$

and we can test this statistically since, assuming efficiency, the cumulative residual is a sum of uncorrelated random variables.

Notice that event studies are about information and not asset-pricing models. Presumably the total change in the return, whatever the pricing model, net the impact of the conditioning variables (the market and the industry in the previous example), is simply that portion of the return attributable to other sources of information, that is, to the events being studied. In an efficient market, this would be valid whatever model was being used for pricing assets.

Theory of Tests of Market Efficiency

Given the volatility of prices in the markets and the low predictability of returns, a cynic would surely argue that prices are really random and bear little relation to fundamentals. If this were so, then clearly the serial correlation of prices over time could be zero. But when a futures contract matures, the price must eventually converge to the price of the underlying commodity as determined by demand and supply, which would imply that the fundamental determinants of the market must influence the change as well as the level of the futures prices. The extensive "noise" in financial markets led Fischer

Black (1986) to adopt the pragmatic definition that a market is efficient if prices are within a factor of two of their fundamental values.

I find studies such as Roll's compelling, not so much as a proof of market efficiency but rather as a clear refutation of at least one alternative hypothesis, namely, predictability. But, how valid is the theoretical underpinning of these empirical tests of efficiency? In particular, how compromised are these tests by the extent to which they are joint tests of an asset-pricing theory—risk neutrality in this case—and of efficiency, and is it really the case that no pure test of efficiency can be conducted? Suppose, for example, you find serial correlation or, more generally, some predictability in returns, what prevents this from being a perfectly acceptable predictability in expected returns? Formally, conditional on the current information, the excess return on an asset (over and above the risk-free rate) is

$$x_t = \mu(I_t) + \varepsilon_t,$$

where

$$\mu(I_t) = E[x_t | I_t]$$

and where I_t is the information set used for pricing at time t. We have gone through a casual argument that the mean return cannot absorb too much of the predictability, now let's make that precise.

From the previous information, we have that

$$\sigma_x^2 = \sigma_\mu^2 + \sigma_\varepsilon^2$$

and

$$\sigma_\mu^2 = E[(\mu(I_t) - \mu)^2] \le E[\mu(I_t)^2],$$

where μ is the unconditional mean return.

From the results of the second chapter, for the marginal investor, if we let σ_ϕ^2 denote the appropriate variance or variance bound on the volatility of the pricing kernel, then

$$\begin{aligned}
\sigma_\mu^2 &= E[(\mu(I_t) - \mu)^2] \\
&\le E[\mu(I_t)^2] \\
&\le \frac{\sigma_\phi^2 \sigma_x^2}{\mu_\phi^2},
\end{aligned}$$

which provides an upper bound to the variability of the mean return. Letting R^2 denote the R-square of the regression of the return on the information set, I_t, we now have a neat result.

Proposition 5:   Letting σ_ϕ^2 denote the maximum bound for the volatility of the kernel, we have

$$R^2 \le (1+r)^2 \sigma_\phi^2.$$

Proof: Since we have

$$R^2 = \frac{\sigma_\mu^2}{\sigma_x^2},$$

we also have

$$R^2 \sigma_x^2 \le (1+r)^2 \sigma_\phi^2 \sigma_x^2,$$

which proves the result.

• • • • •

Let's do some back-of-the-envelope calculations with this. Using our bound on the market risk aversion of five times the observed market risk aversion on asset returns, we have

$$\mu_\phi \frac{\mu_m}{\sigma_m} \le \sigma_\phi \le \mu_\phi 5\sigma_m,$$

which implies that σ_ϕ is bounded above by 96 percent and below by 27 percent as was shown in the second chapter. But, the tests we have looked at have been run on daily data and on a daily basis these bounds become much tighter. With daily data, we have

$$\mu_\phi \frac{\mu_m}{\sigma_m} \approx \frac{(.055/365)}{(1+(.035/365))(0.2/\sqrt{365})} \approx 1.4\%$$

and

$$\mu_\phi 5\sigma_m = \frac{5 \times 0.2/\sqrt{365}}{1+.035/365} \approx 5\%.$$

Hence,

$$1.4\% \le \sigma_\phi \le 5\%.$$

Thus, on daily data, the volatility of the pricing kernel and the resulting potential volatility of the expected return is sufficiently bounded so as to require that

$$R^2 \le (1+r)^2 \sigma_\phi^2 \le (1+.035/365)^2 0.05^2 \approx 0.0025 = 0.25\%.$$

This means that any test of efficient markets run on daily data should not be expected to do better than $\frac{1}{4}$ of 1 percent in its R^2. Thus, any simple test of, say, serial correlation, that does not specify a particular asset-pricing model will still be capable of rejecting the efficient market hypothesis if it merely produces an explanatory power in excess of, say, 1 percent. If it did so, then it would not be possible to attribute the result to the changing expected return on the asset.

On weekly data the results are weaker but still impressive. With weekly data the bounds become

$$3.89\% \leq \sigma_\phi \leq 13.8\%,$$

and the bound on R^2 becomes

$$R^2 \leq (1+r)^2 \sigma_\phi^2 \leq (1+.035/52)^2 0.138^2 \approx 1.9\%,$$

which is still useful for empirical work.

To some extent, then, this also answers Roll's lament over the low R-square that he finds, when only weather should matter. In fact, in an efficient market there is not much predictability in returns, and we should find low explanatory power. To do otherwise would produce returns that are simply too desirable from the perspective of the marginal investor. Of course, it doesn't tell us why—after the fact—we still cannot explain what caused the returns to be what they were, in other words, the unexplained portion remains unexplained.

It's useful to pursue further this argument about a deal being too good. As we saw in the second chapter, there is a growing literature on situations where deals, while not true arbitrage opportunities, are nevertheless just too good to be true. Such an argument was used to provide a formal proof of the Arbitrage Pricing Theory (APT) (Ross 1976a) and it was cast in terms of a high Sharpe ratio. As was noted, however, doing so has problems with consistency with NA, and we moved toward examining monotone utility functions (see Bernardo and Ledoit 2000).

In a complete market these issues become moot because we can actually compute the pricing kernel. More generally, though, in an incomplete market, there is a hierarchy that appeals to me. If we let Φ denote the set of admissible kernels, then our upper bound provides a restriction to a smaller set,

$$\Phi_k = \{\varphi \mid \varphi \in \Phi, \sigma_\varphi \leq k\}.$$

Obviously, if a deal or asset is scalable, then it had better be priced so as not to admit arbitrage, that is, NA holds. What do we make of a deal that does not admit of arbitrage, but looks very appealing? In other words, suppose that for some x, we have

$$E[\phi x] \neq 0 \text{ for all } \phi \in \Phi.$$

If the marginal investor solving the natural optimization problem is supported by a kernel, ϕ, that lies in the set Φ_k, then all scalable deals have to be priced so as to be consistent with some choice of $\phi \in \Phi_k$. If not, then the marginal investor and all inframarginal ones, as well, would find the investment to be so appealing that demand would be effectively infinite. But, suppose that the upper bound on the volatility of the pricing kernel and the attendant upper bound on the marginal agent's risk aversion is too high to be useful, what can we then say? To address this question we appeal to an alternative argument.

As a formal matter, markets are clearly not complete. (To see this, we need only take some asset that is orthogonal or a "cut" from the traded assets.) But, that is not the end of the story; markets may be "price complete," that is to say, any new asset will have a determinate price if it is introduced into the market. Again, as a formal matter, this requires that the market actually be complete: since in an incomplete market the introduction of a new asset can change the equilibrium prices from those that prevailed in the original market, there can be no assurance that a pricing bound derived in the original market will remain valid; the very set of admissible kernels, Φ, will change.

But, this seems to me a rather stark perspective. If one takes the view that all of the important assets are traded in the sense that there is no large market demand for some new assets for hedging purposes, then we can say much more. Any new asset will be composed of two parts:

$$x = x \,|\, M + \varepsilon.$$

The first term, $x \,|\, M$, is the portion of the return that is correlated with the existing marketed assets, or rather, the projection of the return onto M. The second term, ε, is the residual from such a projection. If the residual serves no net hedging demand in the market, then the usual "cutting up" diversification argument will cause it to be eliminated. In other words, while there may well exist acceptable kernels, ϕ, such that have

$$E[\phi x] = E[\phi(x|M)] + E[\phi \varepsilon] \neq 0,$$

hedging out the market component in x and cutting up the residual into small pieces by allowing agents to purchase bits of it would effectively result in sure bets for each individual. An individual with current random wealth, w, would, at the margin for small δ, gain

$$E[U'(w)\delta x] = \delta \lambda E[\phi_U x] > 0$$

from purchasing δ of the asset where δ has the same sign as $E[\phi_U x]$. To prevent this we must have the projection priced correctly:

$$E[U'(w)x] = \lambda E[\varphi_U x] = \lambda E[\varphi_U(x|M)] = 0$$

and

$$E[U'(w)\varepsilon] = E[\phi_U\varepsilon] = 0.$$

The latter term comes from the observation that insurance as a fair bet that is not associated with any of the marketed assets must have zero value, that is, it must be fairly priced.

Summing up, even in an incomplete market with an indeterminate pricing kernel, any proposed asset will have a determinate price, namely the value of its projection onto the marketed assets. The key to this is the ability to insure away the residual, which turns on the claim that the asset offers no hedging possibilities that would disturb the existing equilibrium. This is not, however, an unexceptional view. Shiller (1993), for example, argues forcefully that the markets are inadequate for hedging many important macroeconomic risks, such as employment risk, and that the introduction of such assets would dramatically alter the equilibrium risk sharing.

I am a skeptic about such arguments. If an asset would have an important impact on risk sharing, then it would be much demanded, and, if that were the case, it is difficult to see why individuals couldn't prosper by offering it. Since there is surely no lack of ingenuity on the part of the participants in the financial market, I suspect, there is a lack of interest. It is a bit like the introduction of the inflation indexed bonds by the U.S. Treasury, "TIPS."

The U.S. Treasury, and most economists, thought that TIPS was a wonderful idea, and the market reacted with a big yawn. A much better product would have been a floating rate bond geared to the T-bill rate; it would fit into money market funds and avoid the need for the roll, which, after all, was the way the market could achieve inflation protection in the first place. In other words, the market already had the hedge and would have welcomed a lower cost way of doing it, but the improvement would be marginal, and certainly would not alter the equilibrium in any significant way. Interestingly for our main point, we had no direct inflation hedges before the indexed bonds were issued, but one would be hard pressed to find that they have altered existing equilibrium asset prices in any significant or measurable fashion.

Some Skeptical Empirical Perspectives on Efficient Markets

Volatility Tests

Among the tests of market efficiency that seem most free from the choice of a particular asset-pricing model are the ones that stem from the observation that asset prices appear to move too much, that they are too volatile to be efficient. From the Internet stocks to bonds, there is a general feeling that prices seem to respond too much to news and, more puzzling yet, to the absence of news. These casual observations have troubled many researchers and led to a series of what are called *volatility tests* of the efficient market hypothesis (see Shiller 1981; Leroy and Porter 1981; Cochrane 1991). With stock market data, such tests take several forms. On the one hand, they are constructed as tests of whether fundamentals, such as discounted dividends, are adequate to explain current prices. Intuitively, discounted dividend series are much less volatile than prices, but the statistical analysis is delicate since small changes in the rate of growth of dividends can imply large changes in prices and, as a consequence, the price series is close to a unit root series which makes statistical analysis problematic. The jury is still out on these sort of volatility analyses, but despite the casual appeal of the juxtaposition between the volatility of a discounted average of future dividends and that of stock prices, the evidence is not compelling that this violates efficient markets. At any rate, we will look closely at a more canonical example of a disparity between fundamentals and prices in the next chapter.

Long-Run Volatility Tests

Another class of tests that focuses on volatility is designed to look for long-run correlations in returns that might be difficult to find by specifying a particular functional form and, say, doing a regression analysis. The aim of these tests is to be robust enough to model misspecification.

As we have seen, often weak form efficiency is implemented empirically by assuming that returns are serially uncorrelated. This implies (ignoring compounding or using log returns) that the variance over T periods should be T times the average period variance:

$$\sigma^2(R_t^{t+T}) = \sum_{t}^{t+T-1} \sigma^2(R_s) = T\sigma^2(R_s),$$

where

$$R_t^{t+T} = \sum_{t}^{t+T-1} R_s$$

is the return over the T period horizon, and

$$\sigma^2(R_s)$$

is the variance of the return in a single period.

For example, if T is a year and the individual periods are months, we would have

$$\sigma^2(R_t^{t+12}) = 12\sigma^2(R_t).$$

In fact, though, data from nearly all markets strongly supports the notion that returns are not serially uncorrelated and that long-period returns rise significantly more slowly than linearly in T:

$$\sigma^2(R_t^{t+T}) < T\sigma^2(R_t).$$

For example, in the first such study using U.S. stock market data, French and Roll (1986) find the ratio of hundred-day variance to daily variance to be about 90 (see Campbell, Lo, and MacKinlay 1997 for more such studies). They attribute much of the attenuation in long-run volatility to pricing and bid/ask spread errors, but cannot completely explain it. Our focus is somewhat different. Even if we accept the result as being error free, we want to know if it is within tolerable bounds for efficient market theory.

Suppose, for example, that we assume that returns are first-order serially correlated:

$$R_{t+1} = \beta_0 + \beta R_t + \varepsilon_{t+1}.$$

(Notice that since the variance is essentially unchanged for small periods, β is simply the correlation coefficient.) This implies that

$$V = [\sigma_{t,s}^2] = [\mathrm{cov}(R_t, R_s)] = \beta^{|t-s|}\sigma^2(R),$$

and, therefore, that

$$
\begin{aligned}
\sigma^2(R_t^{t+T}) = \sigma^2\left(\sum_t^{t+T-1} R_s\right) &= e'Ve \\
&= \sum_{t,s=0}^{t,s=T-1} \beta^{|t-s|}\sigma^2(R) = \sigma^2(R)\sum_{t,s=0}^{t,s=T-1} \beta^{|t-s|} \\
&\equiv \sigma^2(R)h(\beta,T),
\end{aligned}
$$

where

$$h(\beta,T) = \frac{2}{1-\beta}\left[(1+\beta)\frac{T}{2} - \beta\frac{1-\beta^T}{1-\beta}\right].$$

If returns are uncorrelated, then $\beta = 0$, and $h(\beta, T) = T$ as we would expect. For $|\beta| \neq 0$, though, $h(\beta, T) \neq T$. More generally, we would expect that nearly any pattern of long-run dependence in the data would cause the variance over long periods to deviate from the linear dependence on the time period, T. For the case of positive serial correlation, it is easy to show that $h(\beta, T)$ is an increasing function of β.

Most interestingly, though, suppose that the efficient market holds and that all of the serial correlation is captured by the changing expected return. We have already seen that this implies a maximum serial correlation for daily data on the order of $|\beta| \approx 0.05$. From the previous formula, this implies that on a horizon of $T = 100$ days, we would have

$$\frac{\sigma^2(R_t^{t+100})}{\sigma^2(R_t^{t+1})} = h(-0.05, 100) = 91,$$

which implies that even a small degree of negative serial correlation consistent with efficient markets can explain a significant decline in long-run volatility.

With simple first-order serial correlation, then, the attenuation of volatility over longer periods need not be a violation of market efficiency. In general, though, the pattern of autocorrelation is more complex—indeed, that is the impetus for using volatility tests—and the question of just how much we can bound variance ratios when markets are efficient still remains to be resolved. We know that the expected return is limited in its variability, and so we must see just how much of an effect a little predictability can have. The answer for the general case is messy, but the following proposition provides a solution in the special case where the lagged correlation coefficients are all the same.

Proposition 6: In the case where all lagged correlation coefficients are the same β, then the minimum value of the coefficients subject to the constraint that

$$R^2 \le k^2$$

is given by

$$\beta = \frac{1}{2T}[k^2(T-1) - \sqrt{k^4(T-1)^2 + 4k^2T}\,].$$

Proof: See appendix to this chapter.

• • • • •

Using the upper bound of $R^2 \le k^2 \approx .0025$ on daily data, the minimum for the ratio of the hundred-day variance to the one-day variance would be

$$\frac{\sigma^2(R_t^{t+T})}{\sigma_R^2} = T + \frac{T(T-1)}{2}\beta \approx 81,$$

which is actually less than French and Roll (1986) found.

In other words, if the market were efficient and if all of the predictability were captured in the mean, the hundred-day volatility could easily be consistent with what is found in the data. In sum, then, these tests, while intuitive and appealing in their simplicity and hoped-for robustness, have no ability to distinguish between efficient and inefficient markets.

There are many more such anomalies with return data, but whether any of them violate efficient markets is unclear. Some, however, whether they are in violation or not, are nonetheless disturbing. For example, in their study, French and Roll (1986) document a significant difference in volatility between periods when the market is open and when it is closed as, for example, on the weekends. On an hourly basis, the ratio can be as high as 40, which implies a very significant difference in the rate at which information influences prices when the market is open as opposed to when it is closed. As with the orange juice futures market, when the information is, for example, weather, it is difficult to understand why the market processes this information more slowly over the weekend and such puzzles remain unresolved (see Ross 1989 for an analysis of the relation between volatility and information.)

Testing the Pros

A particularly intriguing class of tests of efficiency are the direct tests of the ability of fund managers to outperform the market. These tests offer the possibility of being constructed so as not to depend on the choice of a particular asset-pricing model. Personally, I always found these to be among the most compelling since they don't rely on the econometrician's ability to find patterns in the data but, rather, on the actual results of professionals who are munificently rewarded if they do find patterns. The first studies in the 1970s (see, e.g., Jensen 1969) quite clearly show that funds tended to underperform rather than overperform and did so by just about their costs. More recently, some have argued that tests with new data sets developed since that time reverse the conclusions of the earlier work and support the proposition that managers add value. These findings, however, are controversial and not generally accepted. One major concern is that the current data sets have significant survivorship bias in them (see Brown, Goetzmann, Ibbotson, and Ross 1992).

Conclusion

While we have yet to uncover a satisfactory explanation of the microstructure of the market, the fundamental forces that drive markets to efficiency are clear. The "smart" money ferrets out arbitrages and eliminates them, and marginal investors are happy to find grossly good deals, and, even if they cannot find them, the market is more than prepared to supply them. When the prices of new IPOs recently went so high relative to the cost of creating a new company, Wall Street was more than prepared to flood the market with new offerings.

Not surprisingly, then, while efficiency, like its first cousin, NA, can be tested, we should generally expect that it is difficult to reject, and that is certainly what an enormous literature has shown to be the case. But the admonishment from classical statistics that failure to reject a hypothesis is not equivalent to accepting the hypothesis, holds here with force: how can we know that our tests are really sensitive enough, and how can we know if significant inefficiencies exist but remain to be found? Certainly, though, if it were easy to "spin data tapes," find anomalies and profit from them, then there would be a large number of trained folks competing for these nuggets. The classroom joke about efficiency is that of the finance professor and the student walking down the hall and coming upon a $20 bill lying on the floor. When the student bends down to pick it up, the professor shakes his head and says, "Don't bother. If it were really there, someone else would have picked it up already."

Nevertheless, we have uncovered some bothersome facts that are difficult to reconcile with our intuition about market efficiency. It is one thing not to be able to predict what asset returns will be since they will depend on news, and news, by definition, is information that has yet to be revealed. It is another, though, to observe the movement of prices and not know why they moved after the fact. I am particularly troubled that contemporaneous news seems to explain so little of the contemporaneous motion of prices.

But, if we allow for inefficiency, how much is there? As a rough guide, the hedge funds listed in the offshore directory through about 1996 had a (generously estimated) average alpha (excess risk adjusted return) of about 4 percent per year. With about $200 billion of funds, that means about $8 billion of alpha per year. Assuming this undercounts banks and others engaged in similar activities by a factor of, say, 2, that brings the total to $16 billion, and doubling it again to account for all the missing other players takes us to $32 billion, which we will round up to $40 billion just to be conservative. This is a tidy sum, but not when measured against a rough estimate of $50 trillion of marketed assets. This means that, on average, prices are "off" or inefficient to about $40 billion / $50 trillion, which is less than 0.1 percent.[3] There should be no debate, then, over whether the efficiency glass is half full or half empty; it is simply quite full.

APPENDIX

Proof of Proposition 6:   Let V be a covariance matrix with 1 on the diagonal and β on the off diagonal elements. We can write V as

$$V = (1 - \beta)[I + xx'],$$

---

[3] There is some thought that this should be capitalized—although I don't agree—which still means that we have less than 1 percent of total inefficiency in the capital markets.

where

$$x = \left(\sqrt{\frac{\beta}{1-\beta}} \right) e,$$

with e denoting the vector of ones. We can verify that

$$V^{-1} = \frac{1}{1-\beta} \left[I - \left(\frac{1}{1+x'x} \right) xx' \right].$$

Thus, since

$$R^2 = \beta^2 e' V^{-1} e \leq k^2,$$

we have that

$$\beta^2 e' V^{-1} e = \frac{\beta^2}{1-\beta} \left(T - \frac{e'x^2}{1+x'x} \right)$$

$$= \frac{\beta^2 T}{1-\beta} \left(1 - \frac{\beta T}{1+(T-1)\beta} \right)$$

$$= \frac{\beta^2 T}{1+(T-1)\beta}$$

$$\leq k^2.$$

Our objective is to minimize β subject to this constraint, which implies that

$$\beta = \frac{1}{2T} [k^2(T-1) - \sqrt{k^4(T-1)^2 + 4k^2 T}].$$

• • • • •

FOUR

A NEOCLASSICAL LOOK AT BEHAVIORAL FINANCE:

THE CLOSED-END FUND PUZZLE

T HE PREVIOUS CHAPTERS might leave the quite false impression that the issues of modern finance have been settled and that no controversy remains. Nothing could be further from the truth. In recent years the efficient market hypothesis and even the concept of no arbitrage have come under strenuous attack by a group who advocate what is called behavioral finance. As Kuhn observed, science seems to progress through cataclysmic paradigm shifts in which an established orthodoxy is undermined by data inconsistent with its predictions until, at last, it crumbles and a new paradigm takes its place. Or, as Samuelson once remarked (improving on an aphorism attributed to Max Plank), "science progresses funeral by funeral."

Apparently not content to view Kuhn's as merely a positive description, some in what has come to be known as the behavioral school of finance have taken it as having normative significance and, at their most strident, proclaim the death of neoclassical finance and the rise of a new finance based on the psychological vagaries of Everyman. (A good introduction to behavioral finance is the monograph by Shleifer [2000].) Two principal related behavioral literatures are developing, and, at present, behavioral finance seems more defined by what it doesn't like about neoclassical finance than what it has to offer as an alternative. First, there are empirical dissections of purported violations of efficient markets or of NA. Usually this involves finding some apparently profitable risk-adjusted return strategy in the stock market (see, e.g., Jegadeesh and Titman 1993 for work in this vein though it is not necessarily "behavioral") or studying two assets that appear to have identical cash flows or "fundamentals" but different market prices (see, e.g., Rosenthal and Young 1990). These are considered affronts to neoclassical or "rational" finance, and explanations are sought elsewhere. Second, in part motivated by these empirical explorations of anomalous findings, models are constructed in which fads and misdeeds by irrational agents put sufficient noise and risk into the world as to make it dicey for rational and even well-financed traders to take opposing positions designed to profit when reason is restored (see, e.g., DeBondt and Thaler 1987, for the empirics and DeLong et al. 1990 for the theory). Together with their limited budgets, this supposedly puts limits on the ability of arbitrageurs to enforce NA or, simply, limits to arbitrage. As one wag put it, "we used to take it for granted that prices were set by rational agents and now the pendulum has swung completely to the other side and we assume they are set by wackos."

But, as we have seen, the central themes of neoclassical finance aren't based on the rationality of the average person. Behavioralists are surely right about one thing, most of the time most of the people do, indeed, misbehave. To cope with this, the neoclassical theories rely on the abilities and motivation of some smart and well-financed investors, and the theories concern themselves with the behavior of markets, not that of individuals. Furthermore, there is a well-developed normative neoclassical portfolio theory to assist individual investors when they are tempted to stray from rationality. From this viewpoint, then, the theoretical need for the average investor to be rational is a straw man. Given the effort neoclassical finance has made to distance itself from preference assumptions and rely on the stronger principle of no arbitrage, the behavioral critique is ironic.

There is not time here to address all of the issues raised by behavioral finance, but as for the anomalous empirical observations, they seem to me to have some or all of the following characteristics:

1. They are generally "small," which is to say they do not involve many dollars in comparison with the size of the capital markets and are not scalable.
2. They are statistically suspect as tests of efficient markets, along the lines of the volatility tests we discussed before.
3. They are fleeting and tend to disappear as they are discovered—a sort of financial version of the Heisenberg Principle (see Schwert 2002 for a nice examination of this point).
4. They are not easily used as the basis for a trading strategy; taking account of transactions costs in the form of bid-ask spreads or information costs and the like renders them unprofitable.

An amusing example is the case of the stock MCI (see Rashes 2001). There is another company that is traded on the NASDAQ with no affiliation whatsoever to MCI, call it MCI2, and it is well documented that its price is highly correlated with that of MCI. Important news about MCI moved the price of MCI2. It is no mystery what is happening; some investors are confused. But investor confusion and silliness is not grounds for dismissing efficient market theory. MCI had a market capitalization of $100 billion and MCI2 had a capitalization of $300 million and a small float. Any attempt to profit from this phenomena, for example, by purchasing MCI2 when it has gone down on the announcement of bad news for MCI, will be small in nature and doomed by transaction costs. This phenomena is statistically significant, but it has the first and last properties in the list, and it may also have the third in that it might disappear if anyone tried to exploit it.

Exceptions to the list are the "big think" views of overall market inefficiency in which the total level of the market is argued to be inefficient in comparison with some measure of fundamental values such as dividends or cash flows.[1] I won't have a great deal more to say about this point, but it does seem to me somewhat overly ambitious. I know I can observe prices, but I have a difficult time observing and certainly agreeing with others on fundamentals, and, so, saying that the one doesn't equal the other is not terribly compelling.[2]

One case, though, in which fundamentals seem unambiguous is that of the closed-end funds. Closed-end funds are simply traded vehicles that hold portfolios of securities; bonds for bond funds and equities for stock funds. Undoubtably the most visible and disturbing characteristic of closed-end funds is the tendency of equity funds to sell at significant discounts from their net asset values (NAV), that is, the values of the portfolios they hold. It is this seeming insult to rationality and the NA principle that we will examine. This and other properties of the closed-end fund constitute one of the most enduring puzzles of modern finance, and, judging by the attention it has received, if behavioral finance has a poster child, it's the closed-end fund.

In this chapter we will look at behavioral finance by examining the closed-end fund puzzle in detail. We begin with a brief description of the data concerning closed-end funds. The next section develops the basic neoclassical theory and intuition of their pricing and briefly examines the theory's ability to explain the level of the discount for the sector of closed-end funds. After that, we extend the theory with a short description of the role of informational asymmetries in pricing, and then we return to present some dynamic versions of the neoclassical theory. Using these results, we then examine the ability of the neoclassical theory to explain the time series behavior of the data. The final section concludes with a brief and biased comparison of the neoclassical theory to the investor sentiment arguments of the behavioral approach.

The Closed-End Fund Puzzle

Financial economists are clearly as unhappy with the discounts on closed-end funds—first cousins to a violation of the law of one price—as behavioral finance scholars seem elated by them. While the arbitrage between the fund and its assets is not costless and is, in fact, widely recognized to be problematic, and while the totality of closed-end funds is small compared to the value of all traded stocks, nevertheless, it is difficult to understand why a collection

---

[1] See, for example, chapter 3 for a look at some of this work in the context of long-run volatility tests.

[2] At times, when they are arguing that the market is overvalued, the behavioral school sounds a bit like the market pundits who appear on TV spreading doom and hyping their personal theories. I do know one advocate of behavioral finance who could not suppress his glee at the precipitous drop in the NASDAQ—especially since he had gotten out of the market in 1989.

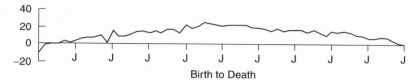

Discount = (NAV − Price) / NAV

Figure 4.1 Stylized life cycle of discount.

of securities should sell at a discount when they are packaged in a fund. A closed-end fund is really the simplest and most transparent example of a firm whose value differs from its replacement cost.

Figure 4.1 displays a stylized life history of the discount typical of the closed-end funds issued and traded on the U.S. exchanges since 1960. Figure 4.2 shows the actual record from 1980 to 2000 for Tri-Continental Corporation, the largest fund traded on the U.S. markets with a capitalization of nearly $1.5 billion (see Lee, Shleifer, and Thaler 1991). Closed-end funds begin their lives with an average premium to NAV of 10 percent when they are issued, despite the fact that existing funds are, on average, selling at discounts. Subsequently and rapidly—within about a quarter—newly issued funds fall to similar discounts. Furthermore, discounts fluctuate widely. The Tri-Continental Corporation discount has been at a high of 30 percent and has even been at a premium of 4 percent during its life. Lastly, when and if funds are terminated—either by liquidation or opening them up—discounts shrink, with the bulk of the positive return being realized at the time of the announcement. Collectively these phenomena associated with the discount have come to be known as the closed-end discount puzzle.

Within the tradition of neoclassical efficient market theory, a variety of explanations for the puzzle have been advanced and found wanting. Agency

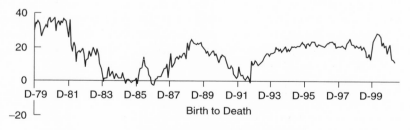

Discount = (NAV − Price) / NAV

Figure 4.2 Tri-Continental corporation discount.

costs, largely management fees, have been dismissed as too low and, since they are generally constant, they seem incapable of explaining either the time-series behavior of discounts or the fact that discounts are unrelated to interest rates as would be suggested by discounting the fees (Malkiel 1977). Similarly, there are tax effects through differential and embedded capital gains in the fund holdings, but these also appear to be inadequate explanations. Lastly, the alleged illiquidity of fund holdings seems difficult to document, and, even if it were the case that funds largely held thinly traded stocks, this would not seem to be an explanation for either the size of the discounts or the rise in price when funds are terminated.

Given the seeming failure of neoclassical explanations, a number of researchers—perhaps in frustration, although occasionally with what seems to me to be a thinly disguised enthusiasm—have turned to less traditional analyses, invoking the closed-end fund puzzle as a signature for the irrationality of financial markets. Lee, Shleifer, and Thaler (1991), building on a model developed by DeLong et al. (1990), base their analysis on the behavior of what they call investor sentiment. Investor sentiment is modeled as a pool of irrational "noise" traders who trade randomly across assets and whose "sentiments" vary stochastically and are correlated. We will take a very different tack, returning instead to the neoclassical fundamentals of NA and to the theory of efficient markets for an explanation.

Our analysis draws on NA to resuscitate one of the failed explanations of the closed-end fund puzzle, namely management fees. Relying on an older and inappropriate methodology, previous research has not adequately accounted for the impact of fees on the prices of the closed-end fund shares, and some analysts have perpetuated the conclusion that these fees are inadequate to explain the discount.[3] The next section develops the analytics of this argument, and the following section develops a simple model in which investors have different information regarding the inherent ability of management to add value to a fund. This model allows for premiums, and the results are robust as to whether or not there are noise traders in the economy and whether or not the equilibrium is fully revealing.

The total discount is the sum of the fee-based discount and the information-based premium or discount, and we will show that this theory and primarily the fee and cost-based discount can, in fact, account for both the magnitude of the closed-end fund discount as well as a variety of other phenomena associated with closed-end funds.

---

[3] Interestingly, there seems not to have been very much research on this point since Malkiel (1977). In fact, not only do many refer to his work as having definitively eliminated fees as an explanation for the discount, many refer to others who in turn only refer to Malkiel—surely an interesting example for scientific sociology. Recently, Cherkes (1999) and Gemmill and Thomas (2001) have made similar observations.

The Neoclassical Theory

Typically, fund management fees are a fixed percentage of the net asset value (NAV) and we will model them as such.

We will adopt the following notation:

A = NAV
V = Fund value
D = Fund discount = $(A - V)/A$
P = Information-based premium
ξ = Dividend yield on fund assets
δ = Percentage management fee
r = Discount rate appropriate to fund assets.

Fee-Based Discounts

Since funds in general fully pay out dividends to their share holders, if we assume that assets grow at the discount rate, then, proceeding with the usual sort of present-value analysis,

$$\frac{dA}{dt} = (r - \xi - \delta)A.$$

Hence, by discounting the dividend stream, we have

$$V_0 = \int_0^\infty e^{-rt}(\xi A_t)dt = \xi A_0 \int_0^\infty e^{-rt}e^{(r-\xi-\delta)t}dt$$

$$= \xi A_0 \int_0^\infty e^{-(\xi+\delta)t}dt$$

$$= \left(\frac{\xi}{\xi+\delta}\right)A_0.$$

Thus, the fee-based discount, D, is given by

$$D = \frac{A_0 - V_0}{A_0} = \frac{\delta}{\xi+\delta}.$$

Importantly, the discount is independent of the discount rate. This is no accident: since the fee is contingent on asset value, as a contingent claim its current value is independent of expected rates of return. Nor does this result depend on the infinite life of the fund. Rather, it is a consequence of the Fundamental Theorem and it arises because of the ability to replicate the fee by a deterministic policy of purchasing and selling the underlying assets. The following proposition displays the full generality of this result (see Ross [1978a] for a more detailed description of the following approach to valuation).

Proposition 1:   If the management fee is a percentage, δ, of asset value, then on a fund with a dividend yield of ξ, the current value of the fees to be received by management per dollar of asset value and, therefore, the fee-based discount, D, is given by

$$\frac{\delta}{\xi + \delta}.$$

Proof: The proof follows directly from the Representation Theorem, but it is instructive to construct a separate argument that emphasizes the role of replication. The manager of the fund receives a cash flow of δA_0. We will replicate these cash flows by an initial purchase of assets and a self-financing policy of subsequent asset sales. Begin the policy by buying a portfolio of assets at time 0 that replicates the portfolio of assets held by the fund. The initial purchase is of a portfolio with a value

$$\left(\frac{\delta}{\xi + \delta} \right) A_0.$$

At each date, t, we will sell off a portion, δ, of the portfolio. As a consequence, our portfolio will decline in value at the same rate as the fund portfolio declines due to the payments of the fees. This implies that our portfolio's value will remain a constant proportion of the NAV of the fund. The proceeds from the sales at time t are given by

$$\delta \left(\frac{\delta}{\xi + \delta} \right) A_t,$$

and, together with the dividends of

$$\xi \left(\frac{\delta}{\xi + \delta} \right) A_t$$

the total cash flow at time t is δA_t, which is precisely what the fund manager receives.

By a similar policy, we could replicate the cash flows received by the fund investor if we began by purchasing

$$\left(\frac{\xi}{\xi + \delta} \right) A_0$$

and, again, sold assets at the rate δ.

Since the cash flows are bounded from below as percentages, they exhaust the total value, and it is not possible to replicate the above cash flows beginning from a smaller initial holding.

Thus, the value of the manager's fee, the fee based discount, is given by

$$D = \frac{\delta}{\xi + \delta}.$$

$\bullet \quad \bullet \quad \bullet \quad \bullet \quad \bullet$

From proposition 1, a (permanent) increase in the payout lowers the value of the manager's fee and therefore narrows the discount. We will extend this result to models where the payouts have a dynamic character.

Proposition 1 applies to a fund that is assumed to be perpetual. In fact, closed-end funds often have fixed time periods over which they are closed and after which they are opened up. Fortunately, the above analysis can be extended to those cases.

Proposition 2: If the management fee is a percentage, δ, of asset value and the dividend yield is ξ, and if the fund will be closed for a period of time, T, then the current value of the fees to be received by management per dollar of asset value and the fee based discount, D, is given by

$$D = \frac{\delta}{\xi + \delta}(1 - e^{-(\xi + \delta)T}).$$

Proof: The proof is similar to the previous one, but since the payoff to the manager ceases at date T, the initial purchase of a replicating portfolio is less. The amount in the previous formula is easily shown to be the correct amount.

$\bullet \quad \bullet \quad \bullet \quad \bullet \quad \bullet$

These propositions can be extended to a case where the dividend yield varies over time in a possibly stochastic fashion. In general, though, the resulting value of the discount depends on the particular dynamics that governs the movement of the yield and its relation to the asset value, as well as on the pricing of the relevant state variables that describe the stochastic dynamics. The mathematics of the above analysis is complex and would detract from the basic theme. One simple extension, though, is to the case where dividends, Y, follow a mean reverting process (in the martingale measure):

$$dY = k(\xi S - Y)dt + \sigma_Y Y dz_Y,$$

where ξ now denotes the long-term dividend yield, S denotes the value of a share, σ_Y is the speed of the process, and z_Y is a Brownian motion.

The total holdings of the fund are n shares and, hence, the NAV is given by $A = nS$. The fee is extracted by management selling shares at the rate δ,

$$\frac{dn}{dt} = -\delta n,$$

and the dividends are passed through to the investors.

Proposition 3: With the mean reverting dividend process, the discount is given by

$$D = a - b\frac{Y}{S},$$

where

$$a = \frac{\delta}{\delta + \dfrac{k\xi}{r+k+\delta}}$$

and

$$b = \left(\frac{1}{r+k+\delta}\right)a.$$

Proof: Once again, since the result is independent of σ, the proof can be obtained by a process-free cash-flow replicating argument that is a simple extension of the ones given above.[4] A more straightforward approach, though, is to set up the replicating partial differential equation for the discount. Since the discount is the value of the manager's fees, we can write this as

$$nSD = nf(S, Y).$$

Assume that the stock price, S, follows an Ito equation with returns of μ and speed, σ,

$$dS = (\mu S - Y)dt + \sigma S dz,$$

where the correlation of dz and dz_Y is given by ρ. The risk-neutral differential valuation equation becomes

$$\tfrac{1}{2}\sigma^2 S^2 f_{SS} + \rho\sigma\sigma_Y SY f_{SY} + \tfrac{1}{2}\sigma_Y^2 Y^2 f_{YY}$$
$$+ (rS - Y)f_S + k(\xi S - Y)f_Y - (r+\delta)f + \delta S = 0,$$

---

[4] Notice that the dividend process has been written in the martingale measure rather than the natural measure. Typically, if the dividends are not perfectly correlated with the stock price, a traditional perfect hedge is not available. For simplicity, we are also ignoring integral viability restrictions between the dividend and the stock processes.

and the viable solution is linear and given by the statement of the proposition.

$$\bullet \quad \bullet \quad \bullet \quad \bullet \quad \bullet$$

Before proceeding, it is valuable to take an initial look at the data and do some back-of-the-envelope calculations if only to verify that we are on a useful track. Table 4.1 lists the fee, expense, and payouts for a sample of funds during the period from 1980 to 2000. For a number of the funds, the data was available only for a subset of this period. From the table, the management advisor fees averaged 60 basis points and dividends and capital gains averaged a total of 9.4 percent.

The fourth column of table 4.1 gives the actual average discount for each of the funds across the years for which data was available. The second column lists the theoretical discount for each fund obtained from the simple formula of proposition 1 for a perpetual closed-end fund with constant capital gains and a constant dividend yield,

$$D = \frac{\delta}{\gamma + \delta},$$

where γ includes both the average capital gains and the dividends, and where δ is the management fee.

Comparing the simple theoretical discount with the average, we observe that while some fit extremely well, there is considerable variation in fit across the individual funds. Remarkably, though, the average actual discount of 7.7 percent across the funds is exactly equal to the average of the theoretical discounts as computed from proposition 1.

In addition to management fees, there are also fixed fees for custody and other services, as well as trading costs, which are absorbed by the fund itself. This ignores the additional "agency" costs that are implicit in any situation involving moral hazard and incomplete monitoring. If we take the view that the additional reported fees are the costs that attend any attempt to form a portfolio, then the advisor's fee is the only cost difference between a closed-end fund and the cost to an outside investor of managing his own portfolio. This augments the denominator of the formula with the excess of the fees over the management fees. The results of this computation are reported in column three of table 4.1 and average 7.1 percent across the funds.

Alternatively, at the other extreme we could treat the other expenses as part of the fund outflow with no attendant flow back to the investor. This results in uniformly higher discounts, and while the numbers are not reported in table 4.1, they average 12.8 percent across the funds. As an aside, these considerations of how to account properly for expenses suggest that an even more interesting puzzle might lie with open-end funds. To the extent that open funds

TABLE 4.1
Closed-End (Equity) Fund Data
(Numbers reported are averages over the data period 1980–2000)

Fund Ticker Symbol	Theoretical Discount	Theoretical Discount (Expenses)	Average Discount	Management Fee	Expenses	NAV ($)	Capital Gains	Dividends
ADX	0.015	0.015	0.107	0.001	0.003	14.408	0.066	0.029
GAM	0.033	0.031	0.088	0.004	0.009	24.019	0.107	0.017
SBF	0.033	0.032	0.100	0.005	0.005	16.234	0.108	0.027
TY	0.032	0.031	0.130	0.004	0.006	28.601	0.092	0.030
PEO	0.025	0.025	0.068	0.002	0.005	21.568	0.053	0.034
ASA	0.016	0.014	0.074	0.002	0.014	47.511	0.058	0.049
CET	0.013	0.013	0.132	0.001	0.005	17.490	0.078	0.018
JPN	0.044	0.042	0.118	0.006	0.010	13.777	0.120	0.012
SOR	0.074	0.072	0.003	0.008	0.010	39.468	0.020	0.081
MXF	0.239	0.216	0.102	0.011	0.017	15.008	0.015	0.022
ASG	0.091	0.086	0.105	0.007	0.012	11.518	0.048	0.021
FF	0.034	0.033	0.078	0.006	0.010	11.674	0.161	0.011
VLU	0.182	0.156	0.150	0.010	0.019	18.978	0.035	0.010
ZF	0.069	0.066	−0.028	0.007	0.012	11.225	0.007	0.087
USA	0.070	0.068	0.072	0.007	0.010	11.167	0.054	0.039
RVT	0.085	0.081	0.097	0.007	0.012	12.872	0.059	0.016
BLU	0.052	0.051	0.062	0.006	0.009	8.394	0.094	0.015
CLM	0.097	0.086	0.164	0.008	0.017	11.385	0.057	0.014
BZL	0.132	0.118	0.092	0.015	0.029	12.703	0.096	0.002
JEQ	0.078	0.069	−0.052	0.004	0.011	10.338	0.034	0.013
ZSEV	0.203	0.177	−0.048	0.013	0.022	8.289	0.038	0.013
Average	0.077	0.071	0.077	0.006	0.012	17.458	0.067	0.027

Note: The theoretical discounts are calculated by using proposition 1. The first column of discounts uses only management fees and the second adds in total expenses.

have excess costs over and above what the market will bear for forming port-folios of different types, their returns should be diminished on a continuous basis. Unlike closed-end funds, which capitalize the excess costs in their discount, open-end funds have to sell at their NAV and bear the costs in their returns. This potential decline in returns would be observable (leaving aside the noisiness inherent in measuring expected returns), but, in equilibrium there will be an identification problem. Open-end funds that pay excess costs would be redeemed out, and the survivors would just pay for themselves—perhaps with a performance premium to cover any excess costs.

Since the overall level of the discount in table 4.1 seems well described by the theory, the next issue to address is what explains the differences among the individual fund theoretical discounts. For some of the funds, the differences are relatively minor, as in the case of ASG and USA. Interestingly, both ASG and USA adopt an explicit policy of paying out a constant percentage of NAV in capital gains—exactly as posited in proposition I—and, not surprisingly, their actual discounts are nearly identical to their theoretical discounts. But, for others, such as GAM and CET, the differences are significant. (Unfortunately for the simple theory, though, ZF appears also to have a constant percentage payout policy and it sells for a premium on NAV!) There are a variety of explanations for this heterogeneity, but it is our contention that in large part the explanation lies with the different payout behavior of the individual funds. We will pick up this theme shortly, but first, in the next section, we will examine a possible explanation for a fund to sell at a premium.

Information-Based Premiums

Presumably when investors first buy into a closed end fund they perceive some value added that compensates for the fees they pay. Typically, the attraction would be that the fund managers are thought to have the ability to add value over passive investment. Models that capture this possibility are explored in some detail in Admati and Pfleiderer (1987, 1990), and Ross (2003). For the purposes of this chapter we will take a more generic approach that is consistent with most such models.

Let θ represent the additional value attributable to the fund management. This is the incremental value that would be added over and above the NAV of the fund. If E^* denotes the martingale expectation operator, $c(s)$ is the random incremental cash flow from the manager's efforts at time s, and I_t denotes the time t information set relevant for pricing, then

$$\theta_t = E^* \left\{ \int_t^\infty e^{\int_t^s r(\tau)d\tau} c(s)ds \Big| I_t \right\}.$$

If it became common knowledge that the managers could add an amount θ to the value of the fund, then the total discount would, presumably, be the fee discount minus θ_t, where we will sometimes use the subscript, t, to indicate time dependence.

We will assume that when the fund is first formed the manager's value added, θ, is drawn from a normal distribution

$$\theta \approx N(0, \sigma_\theta).$$

We've chosen the unconditional mean to be zero so as not to bias matters one way or the other, but that choice will have an obvious influence only on the discount derived below.

Initially, each relevant investor, i, is assumed to have formed an opinion concerning θ from a signal, s_i, which they have received, where

$$s_i = \theta + \varepsilon_i$$

and where θ is independent from ε_i and the ε_i are across investors, and

$$\varepsilon_i \cong N(0, \sigma_i).$$

Closed-end funds are typically sold in an initial offering at which the premium, p_0 is set by the sellers (and underwriters), and investors can choose to subscribe or not. We will assume that the amount of the offering is prespecified. (While this is generally the case, not uncommonly if the offering is oversubscribed, the amount will be increased). Importantly, this process effectively eliminates much of the price discovery that goes on in auction markets and puts each investor on her own. Since the process is not revealing of the common information—with or without noise trading—investors who have received very positive signals have only two choices. They can either commit funds at the time of the offering, or they can wait until the fund trades in the after-market.

Nor is this a simple decision for an investor—even one who is aware that the average fund sells at a discount. That fact must be weighed against the strength of the signal that the investor has received about the ability of the manager to add value. The resolution of this trade-off depends precisely on how the universe of situations is modeled, and there need be no presumption that not purchasing will be the correct response.

An investor will subscribe to the offering only if he or she believes that the post-offering price will not surely fall below the offering price. Per dollar of NAV, the investor must pay

$$1 + p_0$$

to subscribe to the offering. After the offering period, if θ denotes the market assessment of incremental value (θ might be revealed to the market directly through trading or indirectly through revelation of the amount subscribed to, noisily or exactly), then the fund will sell for

$$1 + \theta - D,$$

that is, the information-based premium, θ, less the fee discount, D, per dollar of NAV. Thus, ignoring risk aversion, investor i will be willing to subscribe if

$$E^*\{\theta - D | s_i\} > p_0$$

and, if taking D to be nonstochastic,

$$p_0 + D < E^*\{\theta | s_i\} = \beta(\theta + \varepsilon_i),$$

where

$$\beta = \frac{\sigma_\theta^2}{\sigma_\theta^2 + \sigma_\varepsilon^2}.$$

It is easy to see that the proportion of investors who subscribe depends on θ and is fully revealing of θ. After the offering period, when secondary market-trading commences, θ will represent the market's assessment of the manager's value added. Thus, either through trading or through revealing the initial subscription, θ may be fully revealed, or, if there is noise or if the proportion is unknown, revelation may only be partial.

It is of independent interest to observe that this rather standard offering process is, perhaps by design, one that eliminates information revelation. Except for the possibility that the offer will be withdrawn if undersubscribed, there is no inference about true value that the investor can make from the mere fact that the offering was successful. Notice, too, that there was no need to condition on the success of the offering since withdrawing from an unsuccessful offering is assumed to be costless.

Modeling the post-offering value of the information premium would take us beyond the scope of this chapter and into the area of intertemporal rational expectations modeling under asymmetric information. This is a largely unsettled area and clearly a subject on its own. Nevertheless, for our purposes we can observe that the value of the premium will change over time in response to changing assessments of the managerial value.

Dynamic Distribution Policies

The dynamic realization and distribution policies followed by managers vary considerably across funds. Funds with large discounts will be targets for takeovers, and to defend against this possibility managers may increase the payouts.

Conversely, we would expect that managers of funds with narrow discounts or premiums might attempt to decrease their payouts, for example, raising fees or issuing more shares in the case of a premium. It is important to distinguish between the payout policy and the actual payouts. The policy is the payout function that specifies how the payouts are determined as a function of the underlying exogenous variables such as market movements. Given the exogenous variables, the payout function determines the actual payouts. The discount depends on the payout policy, not on the actual payouts, and, presumably, the rational manager would maximize the value of the discount—insofar as it is the value of the managerial fee. In an equilibrium, the market properly anticipates the payout policy. In this section we will present some simple dynamic models in which the payout policy is fixed and the discount is determined by a market that knows the policy and assumes that it is fixed. We do not go the extra step of searching for the managerial optimum policy, in part, because fund idiosyncracies mean that the optimum policy will differ fund by fund. The models will highlight the extent to which the discount depends upon the policy function adopted by the management, which, in turn, results in the cash flow to the investor.

Suppose, first, that management's policy for passing out gains is a function of both its NAV and of its discount. If the management is sensitive to the discount—perhaps because a high discount will lead to shareholder discord, which will threaten the management contract—then they might adopt a policy of increasing distributions when the discount increases. We could model this as

$$C = \alpha + \beta \left(\frac{f}{nS} \right),$$

where C is the rate of capital gains distribution, f is the value of the discount, and α and β are positive constants. To realize this distribution policy as well as paying the percentage management fee, δ, management must sell the share holdings of the fund at the rate

$$\frac{dn}{dt} = -\delta n - \left[\alpha + \beta \left(\frac{f}{nS} \right) \right] n.$$

The usual assumption that the share price, s, follows a lognormal diffusion results in the risk-neutral valuation differential equation for the value of the discount, f:

$$\tfrac{1}{2}\sigma_s^2 s^2 f_{ss} + (rs - \xi s)f_s - \left(\delta + \alpha + \beta \left[\frac{f}{ns} \right] \right) n f_n + \delta ns - rf = 0.$$

Making use of the homogeneity in n, value will also be homogeneous and given by

$$f = ng(S).$$

The equation reduces to

$$\tfrac{1}{2}\sigma_s^2 s^2 g_{ss} + (rs - \xi s)g_s - \left(\delta + \alpha + \beta\left[\frac{g}{s}\right]\right)g + \delta s - rg = 0,$$

which has a simple linear solution given in the next proposition.

Proposition 4: With a constant dividend yield, ξ, share sales to pay expenses and capital gains as described above, the discount is given by

$$D = \frac{f}{nS} = \frac{\sqrt{(\alpha + \xi + \delta)^2 + 4\beta\delta} - (\alpha + \xi + \delta)}{2\beta}.$$

Proof: Obtained by verifying that SD satisfies the required differential equation.

• • • • •

That the discount in proposition 4 is constant reflects a simplification in the model that prevents it from fully capturing the dynamic situation of the feedback from discounts to capital gains and back to discounts. More generally, the discount is a function of the history of capital gains, which investors use to project the actual capital gains policy. On the other hand, the discount itself is determined by the capital gains policy. The equilibrium in this situation is a fixed point where the discount conforms to the capital gains policy and, conversely, the capital gains policy is consistent with the observed discount. The simple model of proposition 4 bypasses the dynamics to go straight to the equilibrium. With the linear adjustment of the current capital gains to the current discount, the equilibrium fixes the discount and the capital gains as given in proposition 4.

Notice that as the adjustment coefficient, β, approaches zero, the discount in proposition 4 converges to the discount of proposition 1 with the investor payouts augmented by the coefficient α:

$$D \to \frac{\delta}{\alpha + \xi + \delta},$$

and, appropriately, the discount approaches zero as β approaches infinity.

At least as a matter of a fund's overall average discount, then, this allows the formula to have the potential to explain discounts that are lower than those that would be achieved by considering the dividend outflow alone. Of course, the α has to be consistent with the observed fund payout policy.

A second example of a dynamic payout policy bases the payout on the differential performance between the fund asset value, S, and the (risk-corrected) market, M, measured by $x = S/M$. Specifically, let the total payout inclusive of the fee and the dividend flow be given by

$$\varphi(x) = \frac{\delta(x+\beta) + \sigma^2 \beta \kappa \left(\dfrac{x}{(x+\beta)^2} \right)}{\alpha(x+\beta) - \kappa},$$

where α, β and κ are positive constants. Notice that

$$\varphi(0) = \frac{\delta\beta}{\alpha\beta - \kappa} > \frac{\delta}{\alpha} = \varphi(\infty).$$

Some tedious computations also verify that ϕ is increasing in x for $\alpha\beta > \kappa$, to capture the intuition that the managers are compelled to raise the payouts when fund performance lags the market.

If M and S follow log-normal diffusions, then

$$\frac{dx}{x} = \frac{dS}{S} - \frac{dM}{M} + \left(\frac{dM}{M}\right)^2 - \left(\frac{dM}{M}\frac{dS}{S}\right)$$

and

$$\begin{aligned} E\left[\frac{dx}{x}\right] &= (r - \xi) - (r - \xi) + \sigma_M^2 - \rho_{MS}\sigma_M\sigma_S \\ &= \sigma_M^2(1 - \beta_{S|M}) \\ &= 0, \end{aligned}$$

where we assume that the fund and the market have the same dividend yield, ξ, and where we have set $\beta_{S|M} = 1$.

With this constraint, the differential equation for the discount takes the form

$$\tfrac{1}{2}\sigma_s^2 s^2 f_{ss} + \rho_{sx}\sigma_s\sigma_x sx f_{sx} + \tfrac{1}{2}\sigma_x^2 x^2 f_{xx}$$
$$+ (rs - \xi s)f_s - (\varphi(x) - \xi)nf_n + \delta ns - rf = 0,$$

and setting

$$f = nSg(x),$$

this reduces to the equation for the discount

$$\tfrac{1}{2}\sigma^2 x^2 g_{xx} + \sigma^2 x g_x - \varphi(x)g + \delta = 0,$$

where σ^2 is the variance of the residual excess return of S relative to M, that is, σ_x^2. The solution to this equation is given in the next proposition.

Proposition 5: With a constant dividend yield, ξ, and share sales to pay expenses and capital gains as described above, the discount is given by

$$D = \frac{f}{nS} = \alpha - \frac{\kappa}{x+\beta}.$$

Proof: Obtained by verifying that SD satisfies the required differential equation.

• • • • •

Notice that the discount is increasing in the performance measure, x, and that

$$D(0) = \alpha - \frac{\kappa}{\beta} < \alpha = D(\infty).$$

Notice, too, that we could choose the coefficient so that $D(\infty) = \alpha$ equals the simple discount of proposition 1 with only dividends being paid out. But there is no need to do so since such a successful manager might even find a way to cut that payout. In the next section we will verify that x, or, more precisely, changes in x, do indeed play a significant role in the determination of the fund discount.

Our third and final example of a possible dynamic payout strategy, is motivated by observing the annual data displayed in table 4.2 for one of the funds Tri-Continental Corporation. This is also the canonical fund studied by Lee, Shleifer, and Thaler (1991). A glance at the table reveals that the NAV of the fund has been remarkably constant over a twenty-year period that has encompassed one of the longest bull markets in U.S. history. This suggests that an approximation to the payout policy of Tri-Continental would assume that insofar as possible they pay out an amount equal to any increase in the NAV above some ceiling, a. Supposing that this is the fund's payout policy, we can derive the theoretical discount as we did before.

Proposition 6: Under the same process assumptions made above, the theoretical discount on a fund that passes out all (positive) capital gains that

TABLE 4.2
Tri-Continental Corporation History

Year	NAV ($)	Discount	Management Fee ($)	Total Expenses ($)	Dividends ($)	Capital Gains ($)
1980	25.72	0.247	0.103	0.154	1.14	1.08
1981	30.10	0.306	0.120	0.181	1.15	1.64
1982	24.79	0.254	0.099	0.149	1.08	2.72
1983	28.17	0.113	0.113	0.169	1.09	0.00
1984	25.29	0.011	0.101	0.152	1.13	4.46
1985	27.05	0.099	0.108	0.162	1.04	2.40
1986	29.45	0.041	0.118	0.177	0.97	6.96
1987	30.82	−0.038	0.123	0.185	0.89	3.73
1988	23.3	0.050	0.093	0.140	0.81	1.25
1989	24.45	0.126	0.098	0.147	0.84	2.55
1990	25.44	0.140	0.102	0.153	0.86	1.60
1991	24.90	0.121	0.100	0.149	0.78	1.80
1992	28.05	0.082	0.112	0.168	0.78	0.70
1993	28.35	0.109	0.113	0.170	0.80	1.80
1994	28.17	0.135	0.113	0.169	0.58	1.90
1995	23.83	0.150	0.095	0.143	0.73	2.01
1996	27.93	0.150	0.112	0.168	0.66	2.72
1997	30.36	0.168	0.121	0.182	0.60	3.45
1998	32.44	0.172	0.130	0.195	0.52	4.28
1999	34.74	0.174	0.139	0.208	0.48	3.79
2000	31.37	0.187	0.125	0.188	0.33	3.30
Average:	27.84	0.133	0.111	0.167	0.82	2.58

would take NAV above a ceiling, a, is given by

$$D = \left[1 - \frac{1}{\lambda}\left(\frac{nS}{a}\right)^{\lambda-1}\right]\left(\frac{\delta}{\xi+\delta}\right),$$

where the parameters are as described in the previous sections and where

$$\lambda = \left(\frac{(\frac{1}{2}\sigma^2 - r + \xi) + \sqrt{(\frac{1}{2}\sigma^2 - r + \xi)^2 + 2\sigma^2(r+\delta)}}{\sigma^2}\right).$$

Proof: The basic valuation equation for the total value of the management fees remains the same as that which we used earlier:

$$\tfrac{1}{2}\sigma^2 S^2 f_{SS} + (r - \xi)Sf_S + \delta S - (r+\delta)f = 0,$$

in the region where $nS < a$. Since the NAV cannot rise above this ceiling, the absence of arbitrage imposes a smooth boundary condition at $S = a/n$,

$$f_S(a/n) = 0.$$

The particular solution is given by

$$\frac{\delta}{\xi+\delta}S,$$

and the general solution to the homogeneous equation is a power function with the exponent given by λ and the adjoint of λ. Applying the smooth boundary condition and the requirement that the value be bounded, we obtain the solution in the proposition.

• • • • •

An interesting feature of this formula for the discount is that it depends on both the interest rate, r, and on the volatility σ. This dependency arises naturally from the fixed ceiling, which together with the current level of the NAV, determines the expected time until it will be struck and capital gains will be distributed.

Since the average NAVs reported in table 4.1 are averages of the post-distribution values, it is not unreasonable to set the current NAV, nS, equal to the ceiling. Using 4 percent as the average short interest rate over this period and using the annual figures from table 4.1, we obtain a theoretical discount for Tri-Continental (symbol TY in table 4.1) of

$$D_f = \left[1 - \frac{1}{\lambda}\right]\left(\frac{\delta}{\xi + \delta}\right) = 0.066.$$

This is twice the 3.1 percent reported in table 4.1 but still considerably below the average of 13.1 percent for the fund. One problem is the formula itself as table 4.2 reveals, rather than having a hard upper bound, the NAV for the fund has crept upward over the period. Taking account of this effect would lower the probability of payouts and widen the discount. At most, though, the discount could go to 11.8 percent, which is the dividend-based discount from proposition 1.

Such discrepancies at the individual fund level can be closed considerably by a closer examination of the particulars of each fund. Tri-Continental, for example, had exceptionally high discounts early in the sample period and a brief flirtation with a premium. Such a swing may well be explained by an examination of matters such as internal fee renegotiations or pricing issues. Without doing so, though, we have shown that dynamic payout policies can accommodate a wide range of observations. Now we turn to a more macro analysis of the data.

The Neoclassical Model and the Time-Series Data

As we have already shown in table 4.1, the neoclassical model is clearly capable of explaining the magnitude of the discounts observed. What about the time-series properties of the discount, that is, the life-cycle of figure 4.1?

Funds generally begin with an IPO at a premium. This is just as we must expect from the IPO model developed earlier, and is only natural given the way in which the initial investors are sorted based upon their individual signals. Aside from the gullible (of which I have no illusions), the fund will be purchased only by those who believe in the manager's ability to add value (or in the beliefs of others that the manager is valuable), and they will pay a premium to do so.

As the fund begins to trade, though, unless the performance validates the initial faithful, the fund must go to a discount to reflect the fees taken out by management. Since most managers have no special abilities, this is the common case. Indeed, even if a manager is generally perceived as adding value, the discount from fees can be so large as to produce a net discount.

Proposition 2 makes it clear that the fund discount must narrow as the fund approaches a known liquidation or opening-up date. Clearly, as the investors come closer to having the NAV, any fee-based discount (or manager premium) must disappear. Between birth and death, though, there is a rich literature on the time-series behavior of discounts and their relation to variables such as market returns. We do not have space here to examine the entirety of this work, but we can make some preliminary observations. Most importantly, we should expect the time-series properties of the discount to depend sensitively on how capital gains outflows are modeled. Furthermore, we should be suspicious of precisely the sort of aggregate studies that we will carry out, because we know that the distribution policies of the funds vary considerably. As we have seen, ASG and USA explicitly adopt the policy of paying out a constant percentage of their NAV. The behavior of other funds, though, is far different. We derived proposition 6, for example, in part motivated by the observation of funds that seemed intent on a distribution policy that would keep their NAV constant.

Turning now to the data, it has been documented that discounts tend to move together, and this is verified in our data as well. Table 4.3 displays the cross-sectional correlations across the fund discounts and some general indices of the discounts. While there is enormous variation across the funds, the matrix reveals a pattern of generally positive relations among the fund discounts. What is more in dispute, though, is the source of this common movement. The behavioral school attributes this to the commonality in investor sentiment, arguing that discounts rise and fall as investors grow more optimistic or more pessimistic. To support this view they argue, among other things, that the returns on small capitalization stocks are a measure of investor sentiment and that after correcting for market movements, discounts are negatively related to the returns of small stocks. Furthermore, they find no significant relation between value-weighted market returns and a value-weighted index of fund discounts.

Perhaps because of differences in the time period or the methodology, our results differ. Table 4.4 displays the relation between the change in the discount and three contemporaneous return measures. Rather than construct an index of discounts, we obtained these results by weighting each fund in the sample equally and performing a stacked regression on the monthly returns. As we noted earlier, there is considerable heterogeneity in the distribution policies of the different funds, and lumping them together in a single index blurs some useful information. In fact, what is required is a detailed time-series examination of each fund, but so as not to get bogged down in too much detail—"don't confuse me with the facts"—we will plow on.

The regression reported in the first column of table 4.4 documents a strong positive relation between the contemporaneous movement in the NAV and the change in the discount. Surprisingly, this relation is positive, which indicates that an increase in the NAV is associated with a rise in the discount. The second column shows that market returns are significantly negatively related to movements in discounts. In other words, when the market rises,

TABLE 4.3

	ASG	BZL	CET	FF	JEQ	SOR	TY	VLU	USA	ZF	ZSEV	BLU	ADX	ASA	CLM	GAM	MXF	PEO	RVT	SBF	vvretd	vvd	chvud
ASG	1.00																						
BZL	0.20	1.00																					
CET	-0.02	-0.02	1.00																				
FF	0.18	-0.09	0.50	1.00																			
JEQ	0.23	0.10	0.36	0.51	1.00																		
SOR	0.58	0.25	0.31	0.07	-0.22	1.00																	
TY	0.44	0.22	0.18	-0.27	0.02	0.51	1.00																
VLU	0.41	-0.37	0.11	0.08	0.01	0.31	0.10	1.00															
USA	0.76	0.51	0.49	0.33	0.27	0.48	0.27	0.27	1.00														
ZF	0.72	0.63	0.05	0.09	0.08	0.50	0.48	0.28	0.61	1.00													
ZSEV	0.05	0.37	-0.03	-0.18	0.08	0.10	0.26	-0.04	0.20	0.28	1.00												
BLU	0.55	-0.28	0.22	0.31	0.00	0.51	0.15	0.51	0.57	0.18	-0.10	1.00											
ADX	0.54	0.35	0.09	-0.39	-0.41	0.47	0.71	0.14	0.35	0.62	0.08	0.11	1.00										

	ASA	CLM	GAM	MXF	PEO	RVT	SBF	vwretd	vwd	chvwd
ASA	1.00									
CLM	0.34	1.00								
GAM	0.34	−0.07	1.00							
MXF	0.14	−0.16	0.26	1.00						
PEO	0.44	0.61	0.11	−0.06	1.00					
RVT	0.66	0.50	−0.08	0.08	0.02	1.00				
SBF	−0.05	−0.39	0.10	−0.08	−0.15	0.06	1.00			
vwretd	0.05	−0.04	−0.06	−0.21	−0.19	−0.03	−0.05	1.00		
vwd	0.69	0.51	0.46	0.29	0.51	0.47	0.19	0.85	1.00	
chvwd	0.08	−0.04	0.03	0.07	−0.01	0.10	0.05	0.06	0.23	1.00

Note: vwretd = value-weighted market. vwd = value-weighted discount index of funds in the data set. chvwd = % change in vwds.

TABLE 4.4

Dependent Variable:	Change in Discount	Change in Discount	Change in Discount	Change in Discount	Change in Discount
Regressors:					
Constant	−0.001	0.001	0.004	0.004	0.004
	−1.562	1.63	4.452	4.452	4.452
NAV return (i, t)	0.317		0.443	−0.024	
	8.921		11.467	−0.951	
Market Return		−0.137	−0.468		−0.024
		−4.693	−10.895		−0.951
Diff				0.468	0.443
				10.895	11.467
R^2	0.136	0.009	0.222	0.222	0.222

Note: This table reports the results of stacked annual regressions of the change in discounts (where discount is defined as $(NAV(i, t) - Price(i, t))/NAV(i, t)$). Different combinations of regressors are used, including diff ("diff " is defined as the difference between the return in NAV and the value-weighted market return), market return and NAV return. T-statistics are reported beneath the coefficients. Results are corrected for heteroskedasticity by using Whites's standard errors, yet statistical significance is not affected even when not taking it into account.

discounts decline. This suggests that the relevant variable at work is the difference, "Diff," between the change in the NAV and the market return; indeed, this is what is verified in the final three columns. In fact, all that matters is the difference, and, strikingly, its sign is positive. In other words, when a fund outperforms the market, its discount rises!

This result is precisely what would be predicted by proposition 5. The fee-based discount depends on the relative payouts received by the operators of the fund and the investors. If investors grow restless about the fund's management when performance suffers and if managers respond by increasing their payouts, then when the fund lags the market, investors can expect to be compensated (bribed might be a better word) with larger distributions. This, in turn, would result in a lower discount. Rationally expecting this outcome results in the very empirical relation we observe.

Combining the information-based theory of the premium with the fee-based discount theory implies that for the overall sample, the fees and distribution effects are stronger than the information effect. By contrast, it is difficult to see what the behavioral explanation for these results would be. Surely, if a fund outperforms, Psychological Man—if not homo economicus—must grow optimistic for its future, and one would expect discounts to narrow. Conversely, when a fund underperforms, my reading of psychology would suggest a pessimistic outlook.

Of course, for this to be the case we must also observe a positive relation between distributions and the discount. Proposition 4 assumed that discounts influenced distributions. Table 4.5 verifies such a relation. Table 4.5 summarizes the results from stacked regressions of discounts and capital gains distributions. Since distributions are generally an annual or semi-annual event, unlike table 4.4, these regressions employed annual data. The distribution rate, CGR, is forward looking, that is, it is typically the January distribution divided by the prior December NAV, and the discount is computed as of the December.

The first two columns of table 4.5 show the strong significant relation between the distribution rate and the discount. The simplest interpretation of this relation is that the discount reflects the subsequent distribution, and that

TABLE 4.5

Dependent Variable:	CGR	CGR	CGR	CGR	CGR
Regressors:					
Constant	0.048	0.038	0.026	0.023	0.036
	15.143	5.519	5.405	5.204	5.09
Discount(i, t)	0.09	0.078		0.04	0.079
	4.600	3.454		1.777	3.445
CGR$(i, t-1)$		0.202	0.526	0.502	0.201
		1.484	6.235	5.72	1.479
NAV return			0.034	0.024	
			2.16	1.432	
Market Return					0.01
					0.633
Diff(nav − mkt)					
R^2	0.072	0.152	0.292	0.304	0.153

Note: This table reports the results of stacked annual regressions of the capital gains ratio, CGR = CG(i, t)/NAV(i, t), on different sets of regressors including the discount, Discounts(i, t) = (NAV(i, t) − Price(i, t))/NAV(i, t). T-statistics are reported under the coefficients. Results are corrected for heteroskedasticity by using White's's standard errors, yet statistical significance is not affected.

when discounts are high, distributions are expected to be high. The third column observes that the distribution rate is also positively related to the return on the NAV when the lagged distribution rate is included. But, interestingly, as reported in column four, when both the discount and the NAV are included with the lagged distribution rate, neither is significant and the lagged rate is highly significant, which suggests some multicolinearity between the NAV return and the discount. Column five substitutes the market return for NAV, and it turns out to be insignificant while the discount is once again significant. Overall, though, the discount is generally significant, which supports proposition 4.

There are many more phenomena to explore beyond what we have examined. For example, to the list of phenomena we can add some new and even more puzzling ones. Bordurtha, Kim, and Lee (1993) and Hardouvelis, La Porta, and Wizman (1994) document that the prices of closed-end funds traded on U.S. markets vary significantly with the level of the U.S. markets and not merely with that of the country whose stocks they hold, and Froot and Dabora (1999) study a similar phenomena. A simple neoclassical explanation of this would be that since corporate actions that threaten the manager's fees would probably originate in the market where the fund is traded, then, not surprisingly, the manager's realization policies are sensitive to movements in the market where the fund is traded. The model of this chapter can be easily adapted to that possibility by allowing for another independent state variable to influence capital gains payouts, but there is more to be done. In particular, we should develop a somewhat richer model of the realization policy that will enable us to use current results to predict future ones contingent on market movements.

If we do so, it is our contention that having proceeded so successfully with the simple models we have constructed, strongly suggests that much of the closed-end fund puzzle will yield to a careful analysis of the payout policy together with a simple information-based model. While it remains to calibrate and estimate carefully the neoclassical model—perhaps fund by fund—it is clear from what we have already seen that it nicely fits the data on closed-end funds. Contrary to the views of its critics, it clearly has the potential to explain both the discount and the time-series properties.

Conclusion

Like the neoclassical theory, the theory of investor sentiment also attempts to explain the closed-end fund phenomena. The basic argument is that individual investors behave irrationally and in a correlated fashion, that is, they systematically "misbehave." Their misbehavior induces a new source of risk for a rational investor, namely that when a fund is purchased at a discount the discount might widen if the sentiment of the irrational investors turns pessimistic. This added risk is a disincentive to engage in the arbitrage that should attend any observed mispricing between the fund and its NAV, and, consequently, the discount can persist. Furthermore, discounts are correlated across funds because investor sentiment is correlated.

Put cynically, if there is a correlation in fund movements to be explained, then one need look no further than to a psychologically motivated correlation in the movements of investor demands and supplies. For my taste, this is theory that cuts to the chase a bit too quickly. There is no suspense here: assumptions and conclusions are precariously close to one another. I like models with a bit more mystery to them. I prefer first to see what can be explained by purely neoclassical arguments and then move on if forced to do so.

As an aside, while we didn't make much use of the information model, except to note in passing that it is necessary for explaining the premiums at which funds sometimes trade, this is not some behavioral argument in disguise. Asymmetric information has always been a focus of neoclassical finance, indeed, that is exactly what the theories of efficient markets are trying to explain. Such an analysis becomes the province of behavioral finance only when it derives its explanatory power from the exogenous, coordinated, and largely unexplained activities of presumably irrational noise traders.

But, beyond aesthetics, how is one to choose between the two theories? For one thing, the fee-based theory is considerably sharper in its predictions; not only does it attempt to get the signs of the phenomena correct it also makes concrete statements about magnitudes. Since it has fewer degrees of freedom in its unspecified parameters, it should be easier to reject in empirical estimation. Most importantly, though, is the question of what the theory does not allow. The appeal to investor sentiment seems almost limitless in its ability to explain just about anything. Once we have jettisoned the discipline of a market in which arbitrage is eliminated, we can reverse-engineer any observed pattern of prices and deduce a demand structure that would support it. Furthermore, psychology is sufficiently imprecise in its predictions of human behavior that it places no brake on this activity. There are studies that say people are overconfident and studies that say they are timid—for every zig there is a zag.

But, isn't it really the case that the forces of arbitrage are limited and cannot always be relied upon? Ultimately this is an empirical issue, but there are theoretical difficulties that must not be glossed over. At the theoretical level, it is sometimes argued that with unlimited horizons, there is no assurance that arbitrage opportunities will be closed in a finite time (see DeLong, et al. 1990). Even more intriguing are the examples by Loewenstein and Willard (2000), where continuous-time models have arbitrage possibilities that can turn arbitrarily against the arbitrageur in a finite time.

This is not the place to look at these issues in any detail, but the models seem to me to have some common characteristics that must be explored. First, they artificially limit the market structure, that is, markets are incomplete. For example, futures markets are often missing. Often, too, they employ overlapping generations structures but never consider the creation of new institutions that might have longer horizons and would be capable of exploiting arbitrage deviations.

It certainly is possible to build models in which two assets with identical cash flows sell for different prices simply because people think that a "red" bond is just different from a "green" bond or that a bond issued by entity A is not the same as that issued by B even though they have identical cash flows—but whether these models can survive creative market innovations and supply responses remains largely unexplored. My personal view is that they cannot. I didn't really know if the Internet stocks were a bubble until it burst, but I did know that the vast volume of new IPOs certainly was an appropriate supply response.

In conclusion, we have seen that a simple fee-based neoclassical argument can go quite far toward resolving the closed-end fund puzzle. This puts a great burden on those who would advocate the need for theories based on irrational models of investor behavior. To the extent that both explain the same phenomena, the basic aesthetics of science such as Occam's razor argue strongly for the appeal of the neoclassical approach. Certainly, to paraphrase Mark Twain, rumors of the death of neoclassical theory are greatly exaggerated.

BIBLIOGRAPHY

Admati, A., and P. Pfleiderer. 1987. "Viable Allocations of Information in Financial Markets." *Journal of Economic Theory* 43:76–115.

———. 1988. "A Theory of Intraday Patterns: Volume and Price Variability." *Review of Financial Studies* 1:3–40.

———. 1990. "Direct and Indirect Sale of Information." *Econometrica* 58:901–28.

Arrow, Kenneth J. 1965. *Aspects of the Theory of Risk-Bearing*. Yrjo Jahnsson Lectures. Helsinki: Yrjo Jahnssonin Saatio.

Bansal, Ravi, and Bruce Lehmann. 1997. "Growth Optimal Portfolio Restrictions on Asset Pricing Models." *Macroeconomics Dynamics* 1:333–54.

Bernardo, Antonio, and Olivier Ledoit. 2000. "Gain Loss and Asset Pricing." *Journal of Political Economy* 108:144–72.

Black, Fischer. 1986. "Noise." *The Journal of Finance* 41:529–43.

Black, Fischer, and Myron Scholes. 1973. "The Pricing of Options and Corporate Liabilities." *Journal of Political Economy* 81:637–54.

Bordurtha, J., D. Kim, and C. M. Lee. 1993. "Closed-end Country Funds and U.S. Market Sentiment." *Review of Financial Studies* 8:879–918.

Breeden, Douglas T. 1979. "An Intertemporal Asset Pricing Model with Stochastic Consumption and Investment Opportunities." *Journal of Financial Economics* 7:265–96.

Brown, Stephen J., W. Goetzmann, R. G. Ibbotson, and S. A. Ross. 1992. "Survivorship Bias in Performance Studies." *Review of Financial Studies* 5(4):553–80.

Brown, Stephen J., William N. Goetzmann, and Stephen A. Ross. 1995. "Survival." *The Journal of Finance* 50:853–73.

Brown, Stephen J., and J. Warner. 1985. "Using Daily Stock Returns: The Case of Event Studies." *Journal of Financial Economics* 14:3–31.

Campbell, John, and John Cochrane. 2000. "Explaining the Poor Performance of Consumption Based Asset Pricing Models." *Journal of Finance* 55:2863–78.

Campbell, John Y., Andrew W. Lo, and A. Craig MacKinlay. 1997. *The Econometrics of Financial Markets*. Princeton: Princeton University Press.

Chan, K. C. 1988. "On the Contrarian Investment Strategy." *Journal of Business* 61:147–63.

Chan, Louis, Narasimhan Jegadeesh, and Josef Lakonishok. 1996. "Momentum Strategies." *Journal of Finance* 51:1681–713.

Cherkes, Martin. 1999. "A Corporate-Finance Approach to the Closed-End Funds' Puzzle." Manuscript. Department of Economics. Princeton University.

Cochrane, John H. 1991. "Volatility Tests and Efficient Markets: A Review Essay." *Journal of Monetary Economics* 27:463–85.

Cochrane, John H., and Jesus Saa'-Requejo. 2000. "Beyond Arbitrage: Good Deal Asset Price Bounds in Incomplete Markets." *Journal of Political Economy* 108:79–119.

Cootner, P., ed. 1964. *The Random Character of Stock Market Prices*. Cambridge: Massachusetts Institute of Technology Press.

Cox, John C., and Chi-fu Huang. 1989. "Optimum Consumption and Portfolio Policies When Asset Prices Follow a Diffusion Process." *Journal of Economic Theory* 49 (1):33–83.

Cox, John C., and Stephen A. Ross. 1976a. "A Survey of Some New Results in Financial Option Pricing Theory." *Journal of Finance* 31 (1):383–402. Reprinted in *Options Markets*, edited by G. Constantinedes. London: Edward Elgar, 2000.

Cox, John C., and Stephen A. Ross. 1976b. "The Valuation of Options for Alternative Stochastic Processes." *Journal of Financial Economics* 3:145–66. Reprinted in *Options: Classic Approaches to Pricing and Modelling*, edited by Lane Hughston. London: RISK Books, 1999; *Options Markets*, edited by G. Constantinedes, London: Edward Elgar, 2000.

Cox, John C., Stephen A. Ross, and Mark Rubinstein. 1979. "Option Pricing: A Simplified Approach." *Journal of Financial Economics* 7:229–63. Reprinted in *The Handbook of Financial Engineering*, New York: Harper Business, 1990.

DeBondt, Werner, and Richard Thaler. 1985. "Does the Stock Market Overreact?" *Journal of Finance* 40:793–808.

———. 1987, "Further Evidence on Investor Overreaction and Stock Market Seasonality." *Journal of Finance* 42:557–81.

DeLong, B., A. Shleifer, L. Summers, and R. Waldmann. 1990. "Noise Trader Risk in Financial Markets." *Journal of Political Economy* 98:703–38.

Diamond, Douglas W., and Robert Verrecchia. 1981. "Information Aggregation in a Noisy Rational Expectations Economy." *Journal of Financial Economics* 9:221–35.

Dybvig, Philip. 1988. "Distributional Analysis of Portfolio Choice." *Journal of Business* 61:369–93.

Dybvig, Phillip H., and J. Ingersoll. 1982. "Mean Variance Theory in Complete Markets." *Journal of Business* 55:233–52.

Dybvig, Philip H., and S. A. Ross. 1985. "Yes, the APT is Testable." *Journal of Finance* 40:1173–88.

———. 1987. "Arbitrage." Pp. 100–106 in *New Palgrave: A Dictionary of Economics*, volume 1, edited by J. Eatwell, M. Milgate, and P. Newman. London: MacMillan.

Fama, Eugene. 1970. "Efficient Capital Markets: A Review of Theory and Empirical Work." *Journal of Finance* 25:383–417.

Fama, Eugene, Stanley Fisher, Michael Jensen, and Richard Roll. 1969. "The Adjustment of Stock Prices to New Information." *International Economic Review* 10:1–21.

Fama, Eugene and Kenneth French. 1993. "Common Risk Factors in the Returns on Stocks and Bonds." *Journal of Financial Economics* 33:3–56.

French, Kenneth R., and Richard R. Roll. 1986. "Stock Return Variances." *Journal of Finance* 17:5–26.

Froot, K. A., and E. Dabora. 1999. "How Are Stock Prices Affected by the Location of Trade?" *Journal of Financial Economics* 53:189–216.

Gemmill, Gordon, and Dylan Thomas. 2001. "Noise-Trading, Costly Arbitrage and Asset Prices: Evidence from Closed-end Funds." *Journal of Finance* 57:2571–594.

Grossman, Sanford J. 1989. *The Informational Role of Prices*. Cambridge: Massachusetts Institute of Technology Press.

Grossman, Sanford J., and Joseph Stiglitz. 1980. "On the Impossibility of Informationally Efficient Markets." *American Economic Review* 70:393–408.

Hansen, L. P., and R. Jagannathan. 1991. "Implications of Security Market Data for Models of Dynamic Economies." *Journal of Political Economy* 99:225–62.

Hardouvelis, G., R. La Porta, and T. Wizman. 1994. "What Moves the Discount on Country Equity Funds?" In *The International Equity Markets*, edited by Jeffrey Frankel. Chicago: University of Chicago Press.

Harrison, J. M., and D. M. Kreps. 1979. "Martingales and Arbitrage in Multiperiod Securities Markets." *Journal of Economic Theory* 20:381–408.

Hicks, John. 1946. *Value and Capital*. 2nd ed. Oxford: Oxford University Press.

Ingersoll, Jonathan E., Jr. 1987. *Theory of Financial Decision Making*. Rowman and Littlefield Studies in Financial Economics. Lanham, Md.: Rowman and Littlefield.

Jegadeesh, Narasimhan, and Sheridan Titman. 1993. "Returns to Buying Winners and Selling Losers: Implications for Stock Market Efficiency." *Journal of Finance* 48:65–91.

Jensen, M. C. 1969. "Risk, the Pricing of Capital Assets and Evaluation of Investment Portfolios." *Journal of Business* 42:167–247.

Kyle, Albert. 1985. "Continuous Auctions and Insider Trading." *Econometrica* 53:1315–35.

Lee, C. M., A. Shleifer, and R. Thaler. 1991. "Investor Sentiment and the Closed-End Fund Puzzle." *Journal of Finance* 46:75–110.

LeRoy, S. 1973. "Risk Aversion and the Martingale Property of Stock Prices." *International Economic Review* 14:436–46.

LeRoy, S., and R. Porter. 1981. "The Present Value Relation: Tests Based on Variance Bounds." *Econometrica* 49:555–57.

Lettau, Martin, and Sydney Ludvigson. 2001. "Resurrecting the (C) CAPM: A Cross-sectional Test When Risk Premia Are Time Varying." *Journal of Political Economy* 109:1238–287.

Lewellen, Jonathan. 2002. "Momentum and Autocorrelation in Stock Returns." *Review of Financial Studies* 15:533–63.

Lintner, John. 1965. "The Valuation of Risk Assets and the Selection of Risky Investments in Stock Portfolios and Capital Budgets." *Review of Economics and Statistics* 47:13–37.

Loewenstein, Mark, and Gregory Willard. 2000. "Rational Equilibrium Asset-Pricing Bubbles in Continuous Trading Models." *Journal of Economic Theory* 91:17–58.

Lucas, Robert. 1978. "Asset Prices in an Exchange Economy." *Econometrica* 46:1429–45.

Malkiel, B. 1977. "The Valuation of Closed-End Investment Company Shares." *Journal of Finance* 32:847–59.

Mehra, R., and E. Prescott. 1985. "The Equity Premium Puzzle." *Journal of Monetary Economics* 15:145–61.

Merton, Robert C. 1971. "Optimum Consumption and Portfolio Rules in a Continous-Time Model." *Journal of Economic Theory* 3:373–413.

Merton, Robert C. 1973. "Theory of Rational Option Pricing." *Bell Journal of Economics and Management Science* 4:141–83.

Milgrom, Paul, and Nancy Stokey. 1982. "Information, Trade and Common Knowledge." *Journal of Economic Theory* 26:17–27.

Modigliani, Franco, and Merton H. Miller. 1958. "The Cost of Capital, Corporation Finance, and the Theory of Investment." *American Economic Review* 48:261–97.

Pratt, John W. 1964. "Risk Aversion in the Small and the Large." *Econometrica* 32:122–36.

Rashes, M. S. 2001. "Massively Confused Investors Making Conspicuously Ignorant Choices (MCI-MCIC)." *Journal of Finance*, October, forthcoming.

Roll, Richard R. 1977. "A Critique of the Asset Pricing Theory's Tests; Part I: On Past and Potential Testability of the Theory." *Journal of Financial Economics* 4:129–76.

Roll, Richard R. 1978. "Ambiguity When Performance Is Measured by the Security Market Line." *Journal of Finance* 33:1051–69.

Roll, Richard R. 1984. "Orange Juice and Weather." *American Economic Review* 74(5):861–80.

Rosenthal, L., and C. Young. 1990. "The Seemingly Anomalous Price Behavior of Royal Dutch Shell and Unilever nv/plc." *Journal of Financial Economics* 26:123–41.

Ross, Stephen A. 1973. "Return, Risk and Arbitrage." Wharton Discussion Paper published in *Risk and Return in Finance*, edited by I. Friend and J. Bicksler, pp. 189–217. Cambridge: Ballinger, 1976.

———. 1976a. "The Arbitrage Theory of Capital Asset Pricing." *Journal of Economic Theory* 13:341–60.

———. 1976b. "Options and Efficiency." *Quarterly Journal of Economics* 90:75–89.

———. 1977. "The Capital Asset Pricing Model (CAPM), Short-sale Restrictions and Related Issues." *Journal of Finance* 32:177–83.

———. 1978a. "A Simple Approach to the Valuation of Risky Streams." *Journal of Business* 51(3):453–75.

———. 1978b. "Mutual Fund Separation in Financial Theory—The Separating Distributions." *Journal of Economic Theory* 17, no. 2 (April):254–86.

———. 1989. "Information and Volatility: The No-Arbitrage-Martingale Approach to Timing and Resolution Irrelevancy." *The Journal of Finance* 44(1):1–17.

———. 2003. "Markets for Agents: Fund Management." In *Essays in Honor of Fischer Black*, edited by David M. Modest. Forthcoming in Oxford: Oxford University Press.

Samuelson, Paul A. "Proof that Properly Anticipated Prices Fluctuate Randomly." *Industrial Management Review* 6:41–49.

Scholes, Myron S. 1972. "The Market for Securities: Substitution versus Price Pressure and the Effects of Information on Share Prices." *Journal of Business* 45:179–211.

Schwert, G. W. 2002. "Anomalies and Market Efficiency." Chapter 17 in *Handbook of the Economics of Finance*, edited by G. Constantinedes, M. Harris, and R. Stulz. Amsterdam: North-Holland.

Shanken, Jay. 1982. "The Arbitrage Pricing Theory: Is It Testable?" *Journal of Finance* 37:1129–40.

———. 1985. "The Arbitrage Pricing Theory: Is It Testable?" *Journal of Finance* 40:1189–96.

Sharpe, William. 1964. "Capital Asset Prices: A Theory of Market Equilibrium under Conditions of Risk." *Journal of Finance* 19:425–42.

Shiller, Robert J. 1981. "Do Stock Prices Move Too Much to Be Justified by Subsequent Changes in Dividends?" *American Economic Review* 71:421–36.

———. 1989. *Market Volatility*. Cambridge: Massachusetts Institute of Technology Press.

———. 1993. *Macro Markets: Creating Institutions for Managing Society's Largest Economic Risks*. Clarendon Series. Oxford: Oxford University Press.

Shleifer, A. 2000. "Inefficient Markets: An Introduction to Behavioral Finance." In *Clarendon Lectures in Economics*. Oxford: Oxford University Press.

Snow, Karl N. 1991. "Diagnosing Asset Pricing Models Using the Distribution of Asset Returns." *Journal of Finance* 46:955–83.

Stutzer, M. 1995. "A Bayesian Approach to Diagnostics of Asset Pricing Models." *Journal of Econometrics* 68:367–97.

Summers, Lawrence. 1986. "Does the Stock Market Rationally Reflect Fundamental Values?" *Journal of Finance* 41:591–601.

Tirole, John. 1982. "On the Possibility of Speculation under Rational Expectations." *Econometrica* 50:1163–81.

INDEX